PATCHWORK MATH 2

SCHOLASTIC
PROFESSIONAL BOOKS

New York ■ Toronto ■ London ■ Auckland ■ Sydney

Design and illustrations by Peter Samek.
Cover design by Vincent Ceci.

ISBN 0-590-49076-1

12 11 10 9 8 7 6 5 0123/0

31

Printed in the U.S.A.

To Mike, Cara, Mikey and Steven.

Contents

Contents

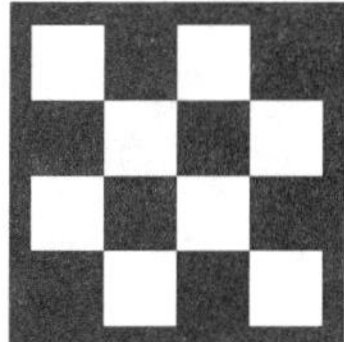

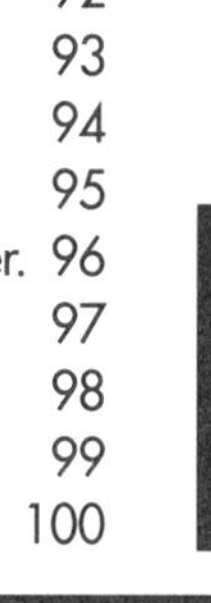

Introduction

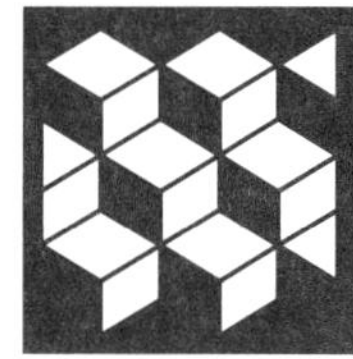

About the Book

■ This skills book provides you with worksheets to reinforce addition and subtraction skills.

■ It also introduces historical background about the name of each quilt design. Each design is an authentic American pattern. Further investigation of the historical period or personage will develop and refine your students' inquiry skills.

■ The Contents page lists each design and the math function it reinforces. The skills are arranged in progressive level of difficulty.

■ Directions for the student have been kept to a minimum to ensure easy use by students of all ability levels.

■ The CHALLENGE (*C*) activity at the bottom of each page is an extension activity that involves language arts, social studies, or math.

■ The creative activities on pages 53-54 and 99-100 allow students to design and name their own quilt patterns. You may want to mount the shape manipulatives on oak tag and keep them for future use.

Class Activities

■ Your students may want to save their completed pages and arrange them on a wall or bulletin board to make a big class quilt.

■ Students can use the shape manipulatives on the creative activity pages to cut patchwork shapes from construction paper or wrapping paper and piece them together to make a quilt square. Several of these quilt squares will make a colorful wall or bulletin board border.

■ Your students may be interested to know that people in many parts of the country still design and make quilts. Your class could choose a hero, a local tree or flower, a national monument, or an important class celebration and design and color a quilt.

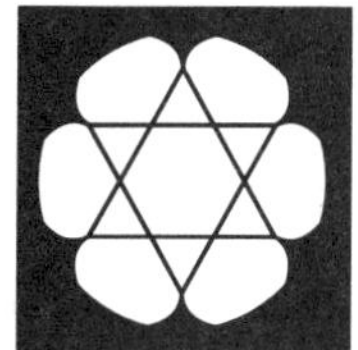

A Short History of Quilting

Quilting is the sewing together of two or three thicknesses of cloth. People throughout history have quilted cloth. Quilting has always served two purposes. Some people quilt to make warm clothing or bed covers. Others quilt to create works of art.

For centuries, people in China have quilted cloth for warm winter clothing. In the Middle ages, The Crusaders liked to wear quilted shirts to prevent chafing under their heavy chain mail. Queens quilted and peasant women quilted. Many designs were passed down from generation to generation.

Quilting was introduced to the New World when Pilgrims traveled across the ocean on the Mayflower. When the coverlets and quilts they brought from England wore out, the Pilgrims mended them with strong pieces of material from worn-out clothing and blankets. These scrap quilts, considered the first crazy quilts, were probobly not beautiful but were very functional.

Naming quilt designs is a custom as old as quilt making itself. Some names reflect contemporary slang, popular sayings, and political activities and customs. Some quilts were named for tools and machines. In other designs you can see trees or flowers or religious symbols.

Many of the quilt designs in this book have more than one name. That is because people all over the country make quilts. The histories given for each quilt name are as close to accurate as possible. When there was a choice of name for the quilt, the one that would most appeal to students was chosen.

The Ladder

4 × 1 | 7 × 1 | 5 × 1 | 3 × 1 | 9 × 1

8 × 1

5 × 1 | 0 × 6 | 7 × 1 | 1 × 2

1 × 1 | 1 × 8 | 6 × 0 | 1 × 7

3 × 0 | 6 × 1 | 1 × 3 | 1 × 8

4 × 0 | 1 × 8 | 9 × 0 | 2 × 1 | 5 × 1

7 × 1

6 × 1 | 0 × 2 | 1 × 5 | 1 × 4

Color:

0, 1, 2, 3, and 4 = blue
5, 6, 7, 8, and 9 = red

Sometimes ladders and stairs look alike. Can you find patterns for both in this design?

***C* On the back of this sheet of paper, write about three things that are blue in your classroom.**

Old Town Pump

Color:

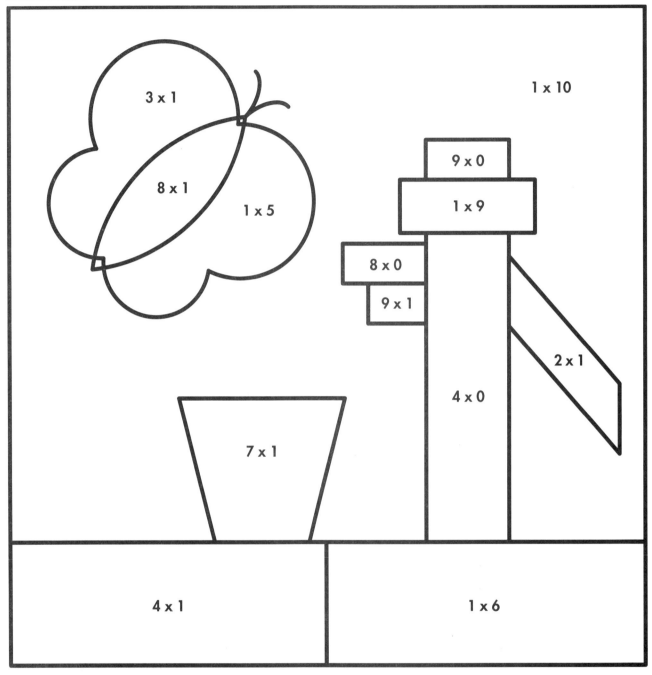

0 and 2 = red
1, 3, and 5 = orange
4 and 6 = green
7 and 8 = yellow
9 = black
10 = blue

There was a time in the history of our country when people got their water from a town pump.

***C* Practice the multiplication facts for one out loud with a friend.**

Mary Tenney Gray Travel Club Patch

x2

5
x2

12
x2

11
x2

10
x2

2
x7

8
x2

3
x2

2
x9

2
x6

9
x2

6
x2

7
x2

2
x8

2
x10

2
x12

2
x11

2
x5

Color:

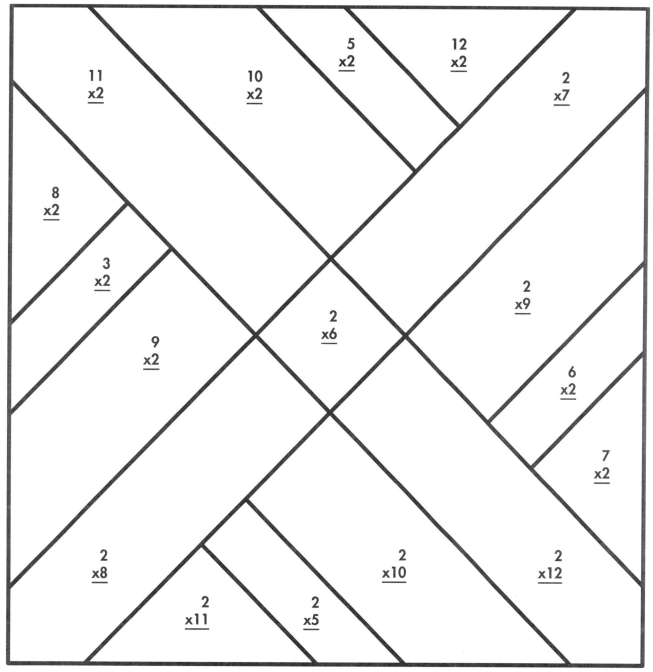

6, 8, 10, and 12 = red
14 and 16 = purple
18 and 20 = yellow
22 and 24 = green

A young girl named this design after her mother, Mary Tenney Gray.

***C* On the back of this sheet of paper, draw a special quilt pattern for your mother.**

x2

Mexican Star

4 x 2 | 6 x 2 | 9 x 2 | 3 x 2 | 2 x 9 | 2 x 6 | 2 x 3

7 x 2 | 10 x 2 | 8 x 2 | 7 x 2 | 12 x 2 | 10 x 2

4 x 2 | 2 x 11 | 2 x 4

$$\begin{array}{r} 2 \\ \times 8 \\ \hline \end{array}$$

11 x 2 | 6 x 2 | 2 x 7 | 5 x 2 | 2 x 6 | 11 x 2 | 2 x 8

12 x 2 | 2 x 9 | 3 x 2 | 2 x 9 | 7 x 2 | 5 x 2

7 x 2

Color:

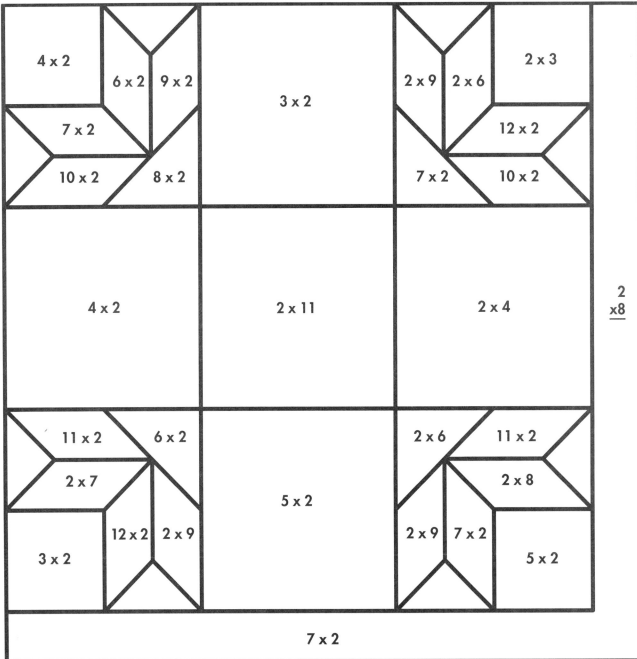

6, 8, and 10 = yellow
18, 20, and 22 = green
12, 14, 16, and 24 = red

Many Mexican clothes have star designs like this one.

***C* Look at a map of Mexico. Then write the name of three Mexican towns on the back of this sheet of paper.**

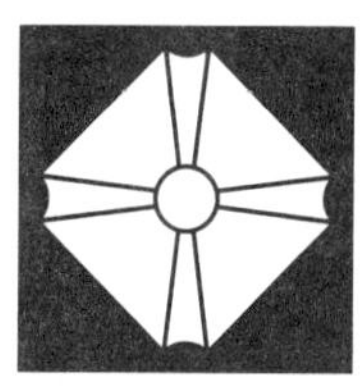

Dusty Miller

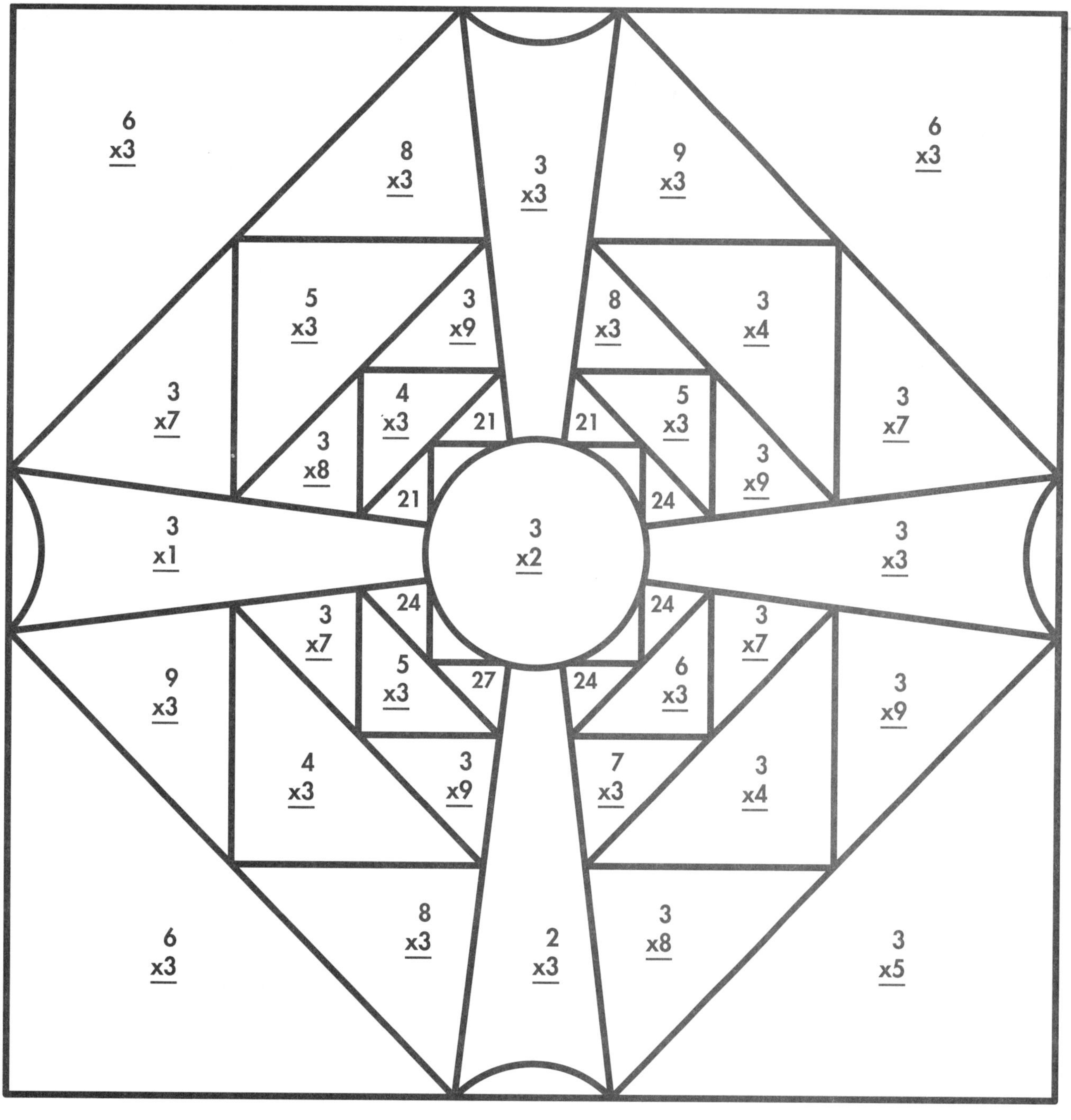

6 x3 | 8 x3 | 3 x3 | 9 x3 | 6 x3

5 x3 | 3 x9 | 8 x3 | 3 x4

3 x7 | 4 x3 | 21 | 21 | 5 x3 | 3 x7

3 x8 | 21 | 24 | 3 x9

3 x1 | 3 x2 | 3 x3

24 | 3 x7 | 24 | 3 x7

9 x3 | 5 x3 | 27 | 24 | 6 x3 | 3 x9

4 x3 | 3 x9 | 7 x3 | 3 x4

6 x3 | 8 x3 | 2 x3 | 3 x8 | 3 x5

Color:

3, 6, and 9 = brown
12, 15, and 18 = green
21, 24, and 27 = orange

Mills use huge stones to grind wheat into flour. The flour makes the stone very dusty.

C On the back of this sheet of paper, number by threes to sixty.

Morning Star

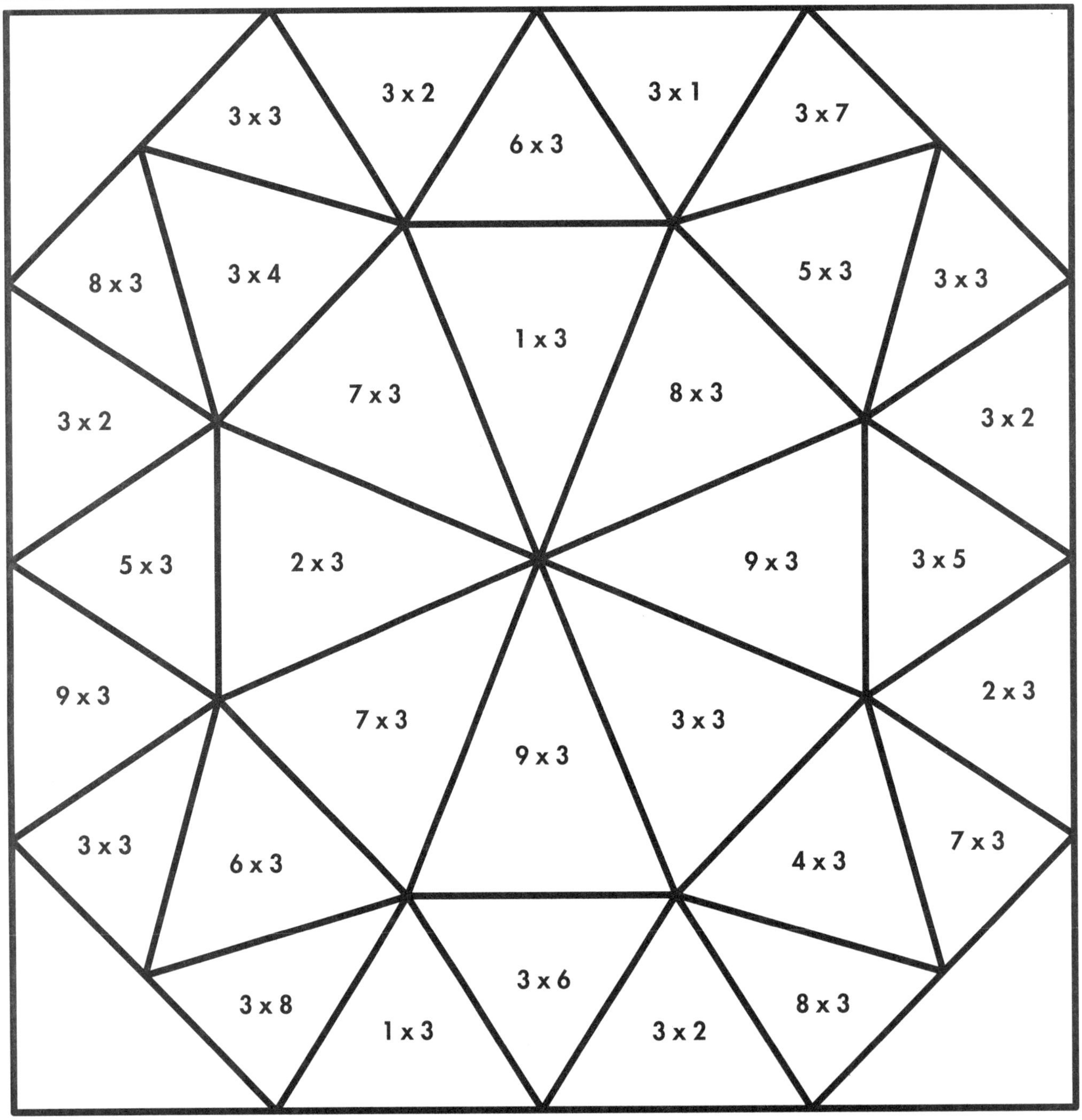

3 x 3	3 x 2	6 x 3	3 x 1	3 x 7	
8 x 3	3 x 4	1 x 3	5 x 3	3 x 3	
3 x 2	7 x 3	8 x 3	3 x 2		
5 x 3	2 x 3	9 x 3	3 x 5		
9 x 3	7 x 3	9 x 3	3 x 3	2 x 3	
3 x 3	6 x 3	4 x 3	7 x 3		
3 x 8	1 x 3	3 x 6	3 x 2	8 x 3	

Color:

3, 6, and 27 = red
12, 15, and 18= orange
9, 21, and 24 = green

After you color this design, you'll see the shape of the morning star.

C Write three multiplication facts that have an answer in the twenties.

Dutch Mill

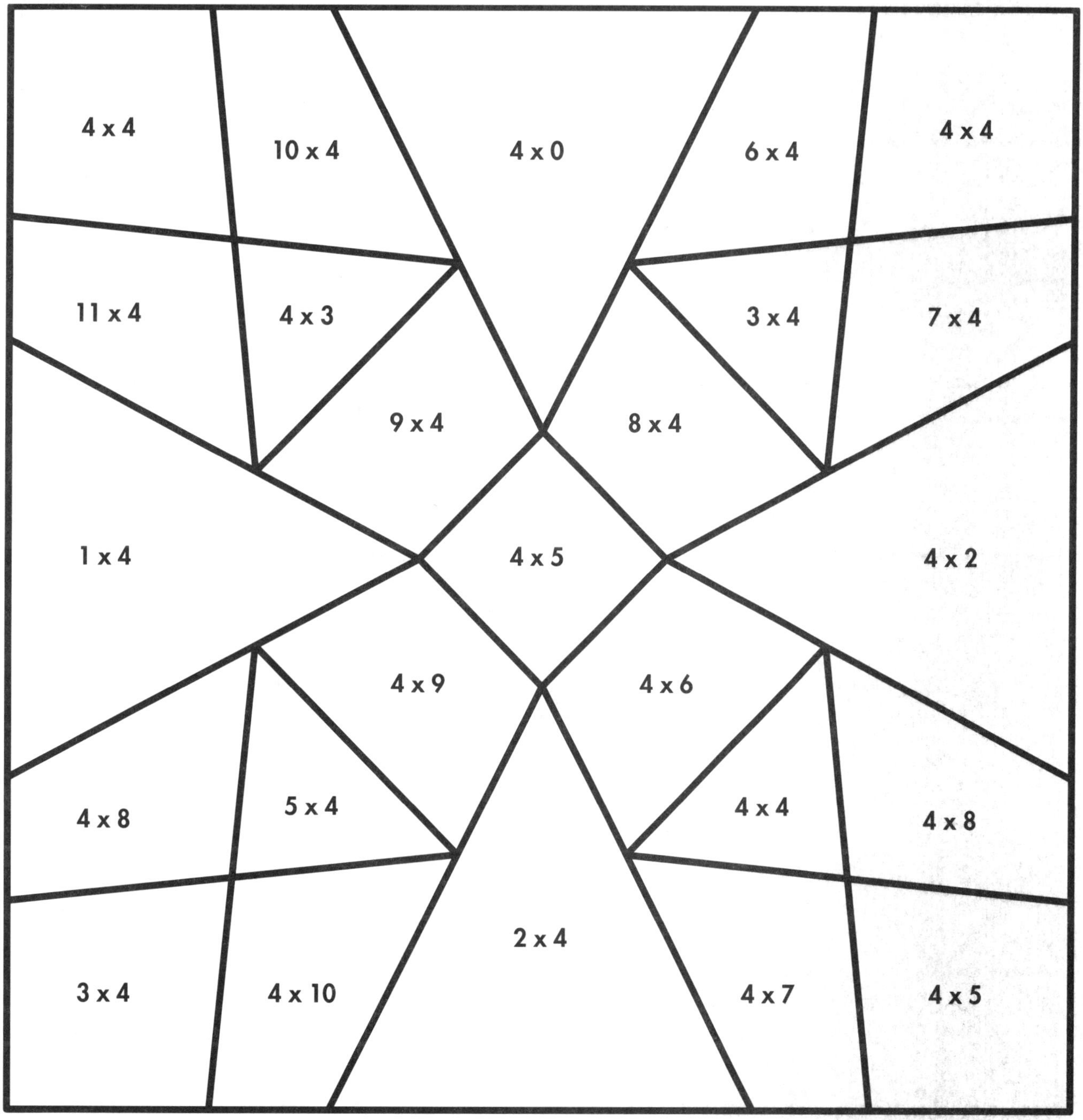

4 x 4	10 x 4	4 x 0	6 x 4	4 x 4
11 x 4	4 x 3		3 x 4	7 x 4
	9 x 4		8 x 4	
1 x 4		4 x 5		4 x 2
	4 x 9		4 x 6	
4 x 8	5 x 4		4 x 4	4 x 8
3 x 4	4 x 10	2 x 4	4 x 7	4 x 5

Color:

0, 4, and 8 = brown
24, 28, 32, 36, 40, and 44 = blue
12, 16, and 20 = red

This design has the shape of the windmills in Holland.

***C* On the back of this sheet of paper, write what you think windmills are used for.**

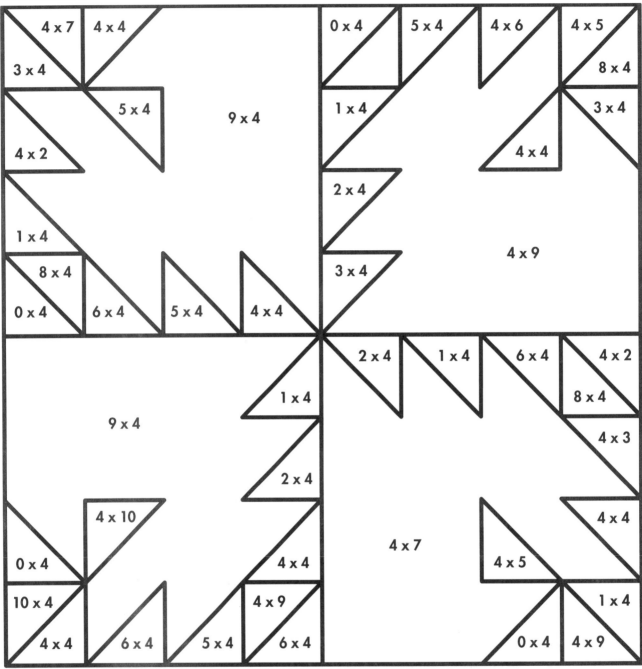

Eternal Triangle

4 x 7 4 x 4
3 x 4
5 x 4 9 x 4
4 x 2
1 x 4
8 x 4
0 x 4 6 x 4 5 x 4 4 x 4

0 x 4 5 x 4 4 x 6 4 x 5
8 x 4
1 x 4 3 x 4
4 x 4
2 x 4
4 x 9
3 x 4

1 x 4
9 x 4
2 x 4
4 x 10
0 x 4 4 x 4
10 x 4 4 x 9
4 x 4 6 x 4 5 x 4 6 x 4

2 x 4 1 x 4 6 x 4 4 x 2
8 x 4
4 x 3
4 x 4
4 x 7
4 x 5
1 x 4
0 x 4 4 x 9

Color:

If the answer is less than 25, color the space black.

If the answer is greater than 25, color the space green.

How many triangles can you count in this design?

____

***C* Underline every answer that has a two in the tens place.**

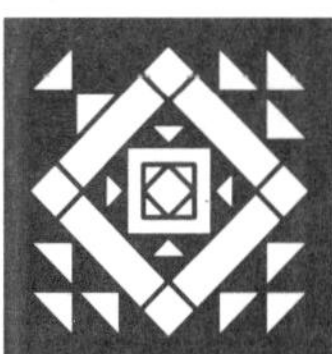

Mrs. Cleveland's Choice

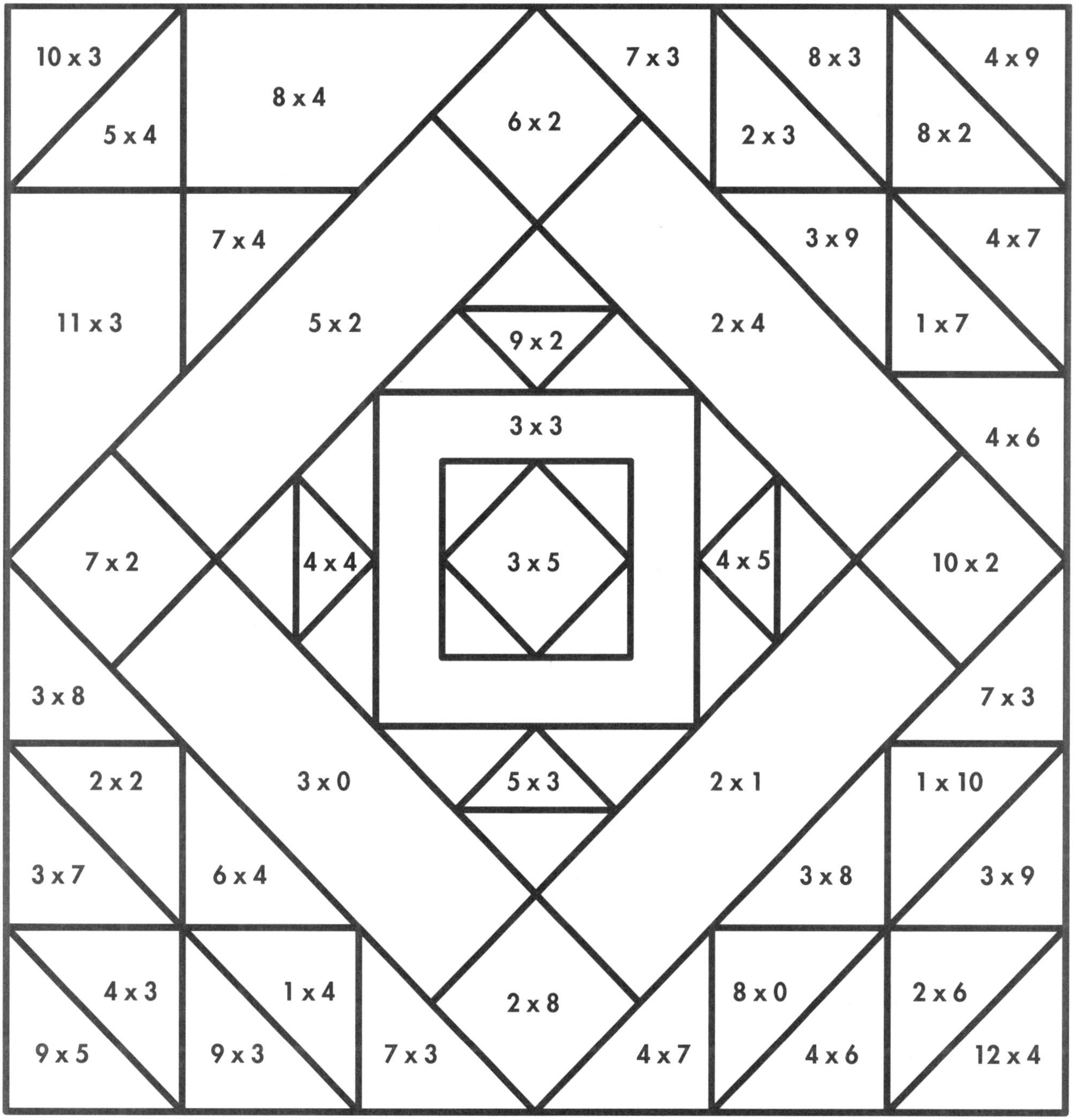

10 x 3 5 x 4 8 x 4 6 x 2 7 x 3 8 x 3 2 x 3 4 x 9 8 x 2

7 x 4 11 x 3 5 x 2 9 x 2 2 x 4 3 x 9 4 x 7 1 x 7

3 x 3 4 x 6

7 x 2 4 x 4 3 x 5 4 x 5 10 x 2

3 x 8 7 x 3

2 x 2 3 x 0 5 x 3 2 x 1 1 x 10

3 x 7 6 x 4 3 x 8 3 x 9

4 x 3 1 x 4 2 x 8 8 x 0 2 x 6

9 x 5 9 x 3 7 x 3 4 x 7 4 x 6 12 x 4

Color:

If the answer is from 0 to 10, color the space orange.
If the answer is from 11 to 20, color the space black.
If the answer is from 21 to 28, color the space green.
If the answer is from 29 to 48, color the space yellow.

This design was named in honor of President Cleveland's wife. She was one of our country's first ladies.

***C* When was Grover Cleveland president? Write the dates on the back of this sheet of paper.**

Scrap Bag

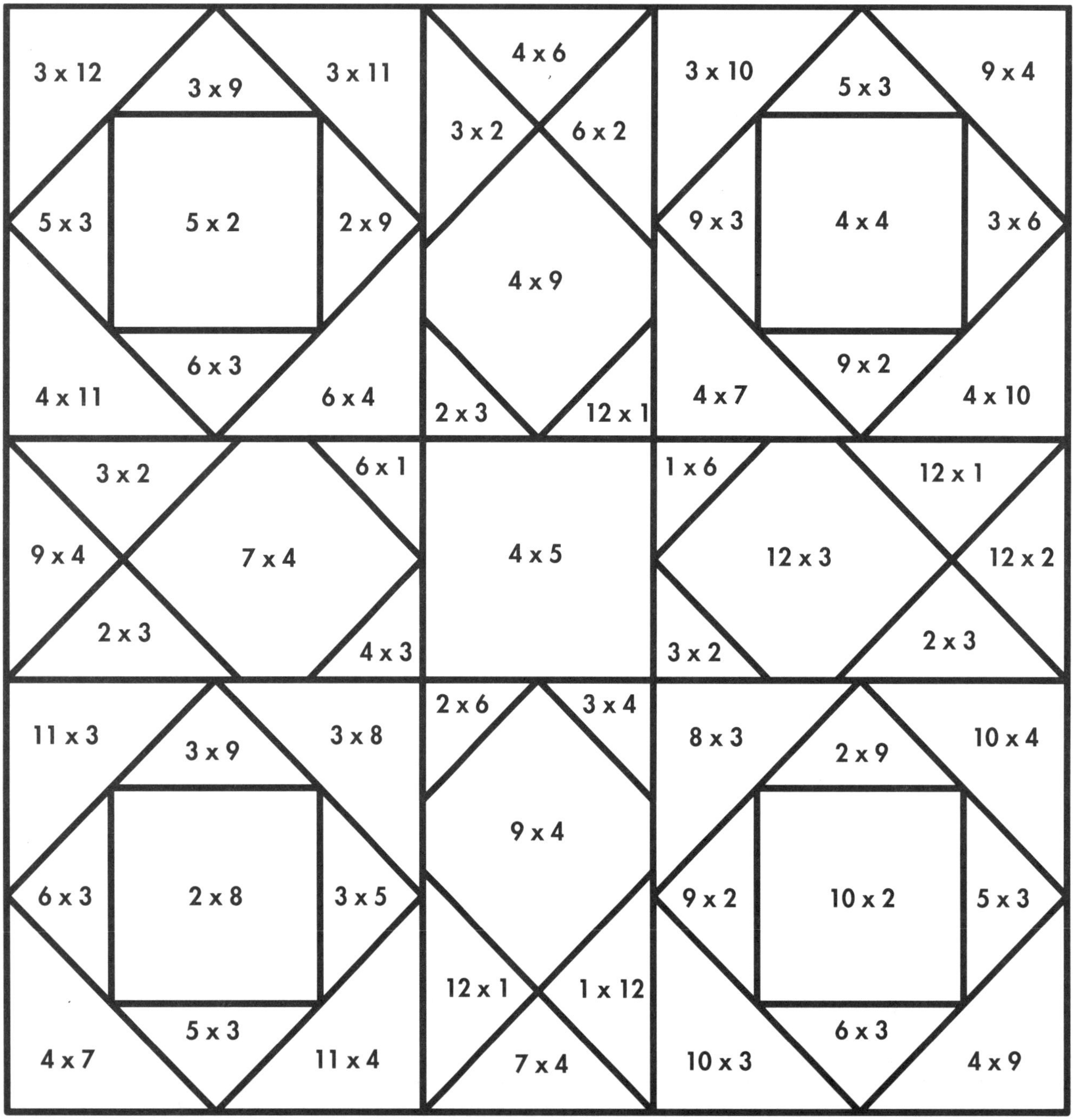

3 x 12 | 3 x 9 | 3 x 11 | 4 x 6 | 3 x 10 | 5 x 3 | 9 x 4

3 x 2 | 6 x 2

5 x 3 | 5 x 2 | 2 x 9 | 9 x 3 | 4 x 4 | 3 x 6

4 x 9

6 x 3 | 9 x 2

4 x 11 | 6 x 4 | 2 x 3 | 12 x 1 | 4 x 7 | 4 x 10

3 x 2 | 6 x 1 | 1 x 6 | 12 x 1

9 x 4 | 7 x 4 | 4 x 5 | 12 x 3 | 12 x 2

2 x 3 | 4 x 3 | 3 x 2 | 2 x 3

2 x 6 | 3 x 4

11 x 3 | 3 x 9 | 3 x 8 | 8 x 3 | 2 x 9 | 10 x 4

9 x 4

6 x 3 | 2 x 8 | 3 x 5 | 9 x 2 | 10 x 2 | 5 x 3

12 x 1 | 1 x 12

5 x 3 | 6 x 3

4 x 7 | 11 x 4 | 7 x 4 | 10 x 3 | 4 x 9

Color:

10, 16, and 20 = red
15, 18, and 27 = green
24, 28, and 36 = blue
30, 33, 40, and 44 = orange
6 and 12 = yellow

Quilters used this pattern when they had lots of extra cloth in their scrap bags.

***C* Write the multiplication facts for four on the back of this sheet of paper.**

Swing in the Center

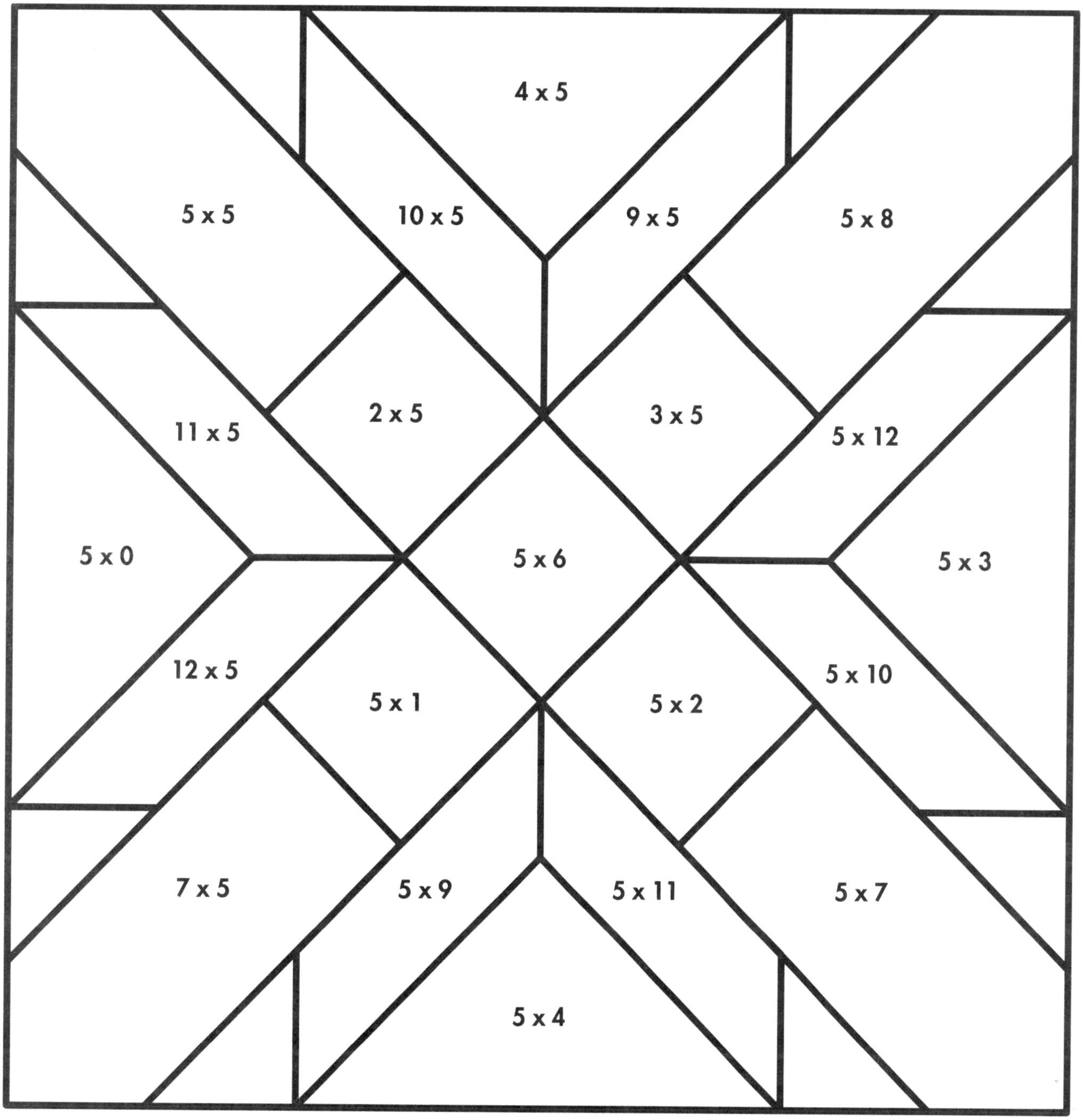

If the answer is between
0 and 20, color the space yellow.

If the answer is between
25 and 40, color the space orange.

If the answer is between
45 and 60, color the space green.

This pattern is named for a direction in square dancing.

C Skip-count out loud by fives to a partner. Count to one hundred and fifty.

Eight Hands Round

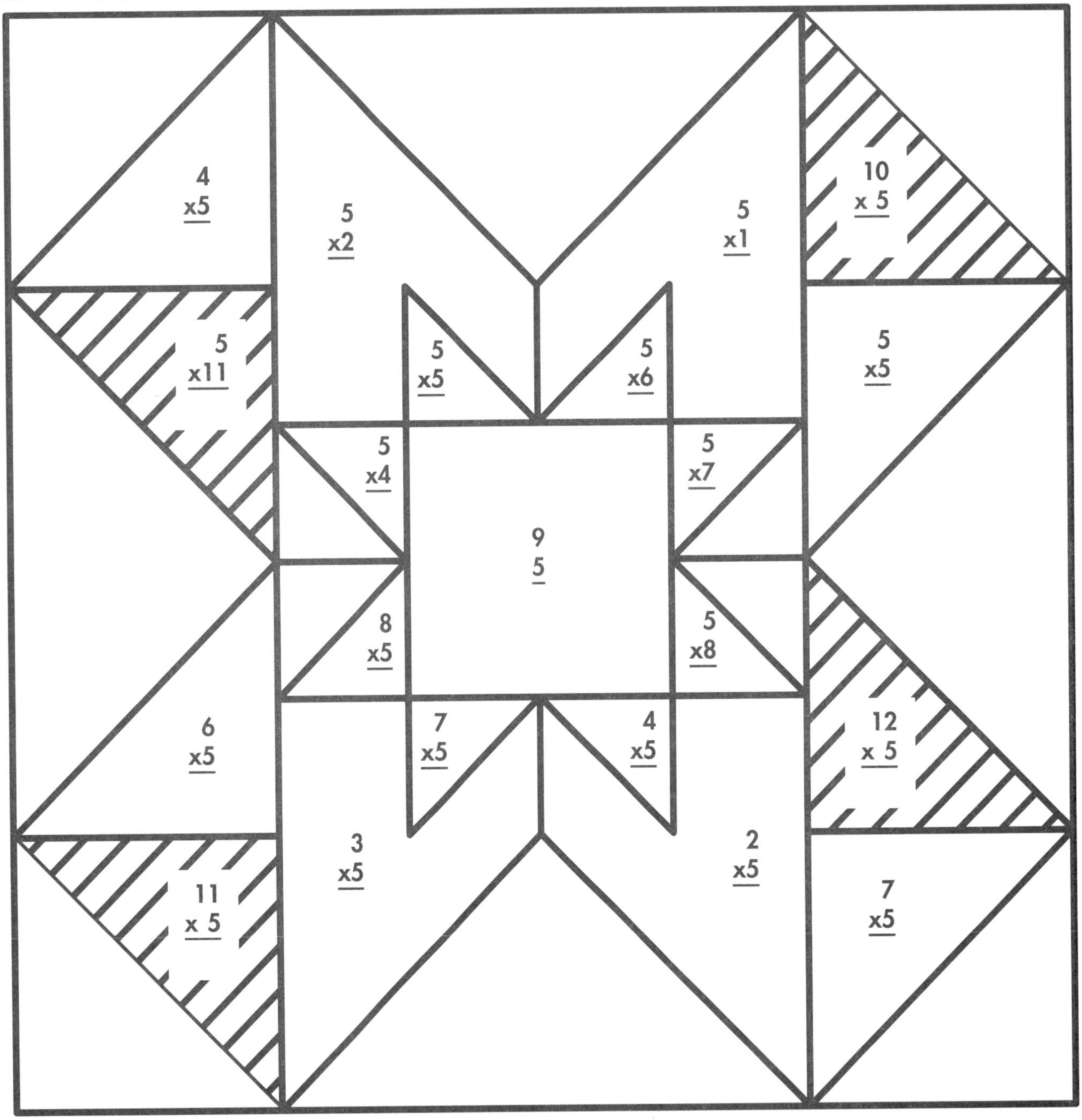

4
x5

5
x2

5
x1

10
x 5

5
x11

5
x5

5
x6

5
x5

5
x4

5
x7

9
5

8
x5

5
x8

6
x5

7
x5

4
x5

12
x 5

11
x 5

3
x5

2
x5

7
x5

If the answer is between
5 and 15, color the space orange.

If the answer is between
20 and 40, color the space black.

If the answer is between
45 and 60, color the space red.

In square dances, people often hold hands and spin in a circle. Can you see the pattern eight people would make?

____

***C* On the back of this sheet of paper, write a set of directions for a dance you would like to do.**

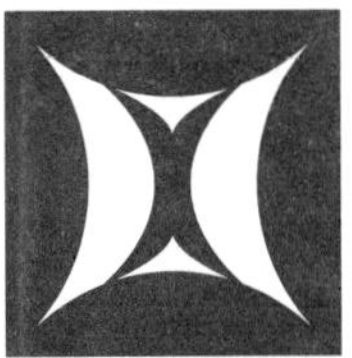

Chimney Swallows

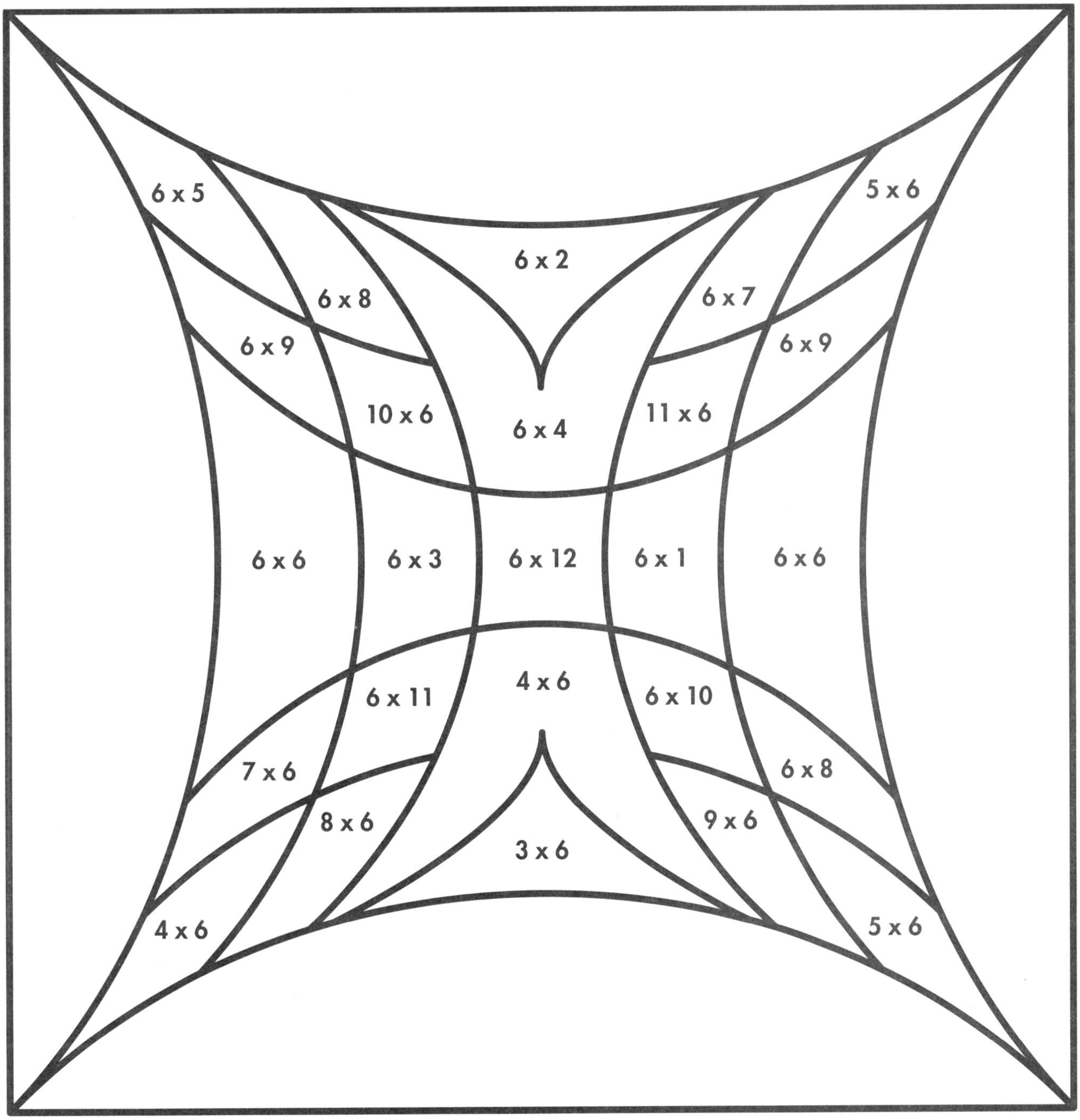

Color:

6, 12, and 18 = blue
24, 30, and 36 = red
42, 48, and 54 = yellow
60, 66, and 72 = black

Swallows like to nest in chimneys. The shape of their pointed tails is in this pattern.

***C* Make flash cards for multiplication facts for six. Practice them with a friend.**

Hero's Crown

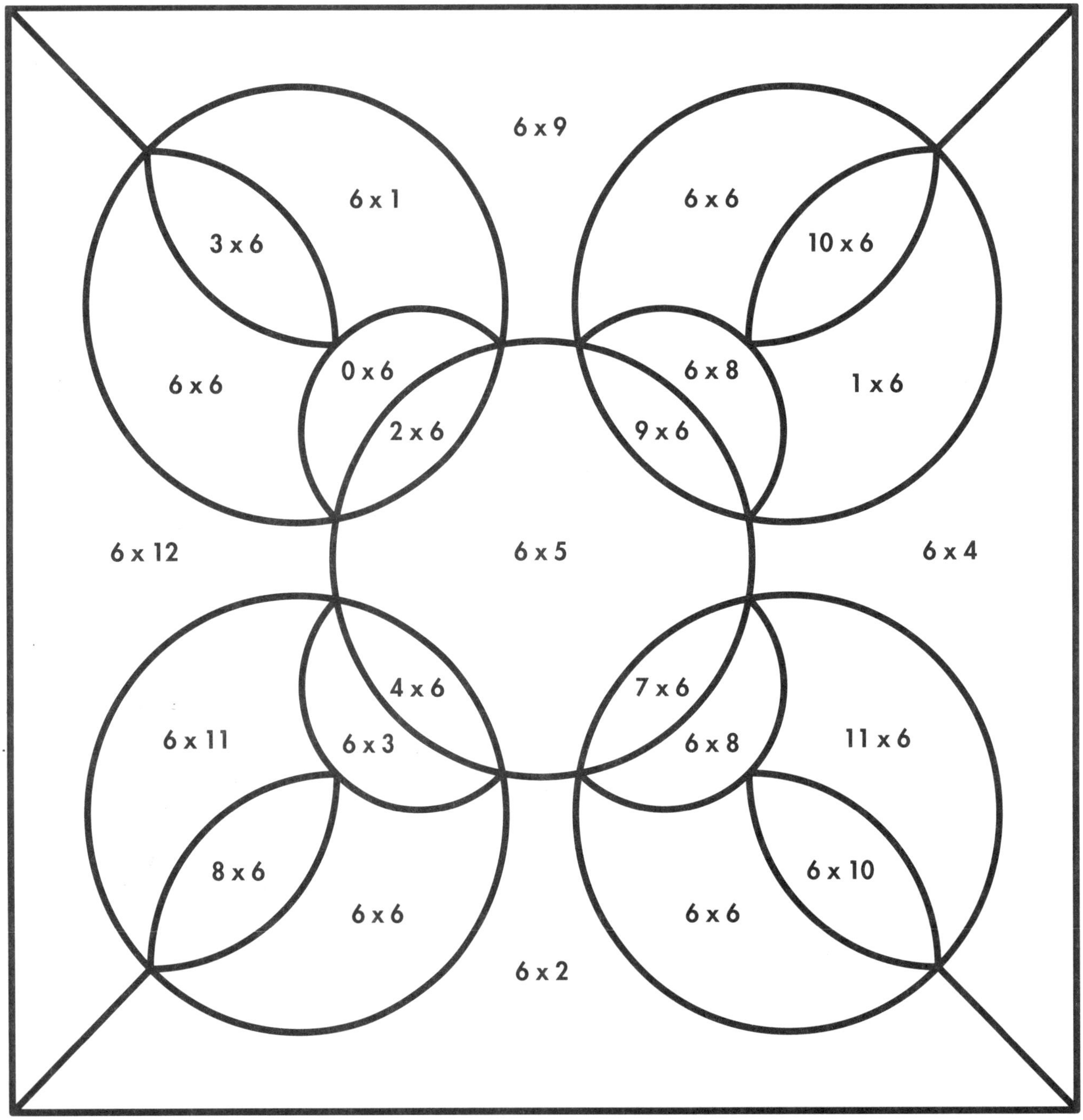

If the answer ends with 6, color the space orange.
If the answer ends with 0 or 8, color the space purple.
If the answer ends with 2 or 4, color the space brown.

Long ago, some crowns were made of leaves and flowers. The quilt maker may have had this in mind when she named this pattern.

***C* On the back of this sheet of paper, design a crown you would like to wear.**

Mrs. Morgan's Choice

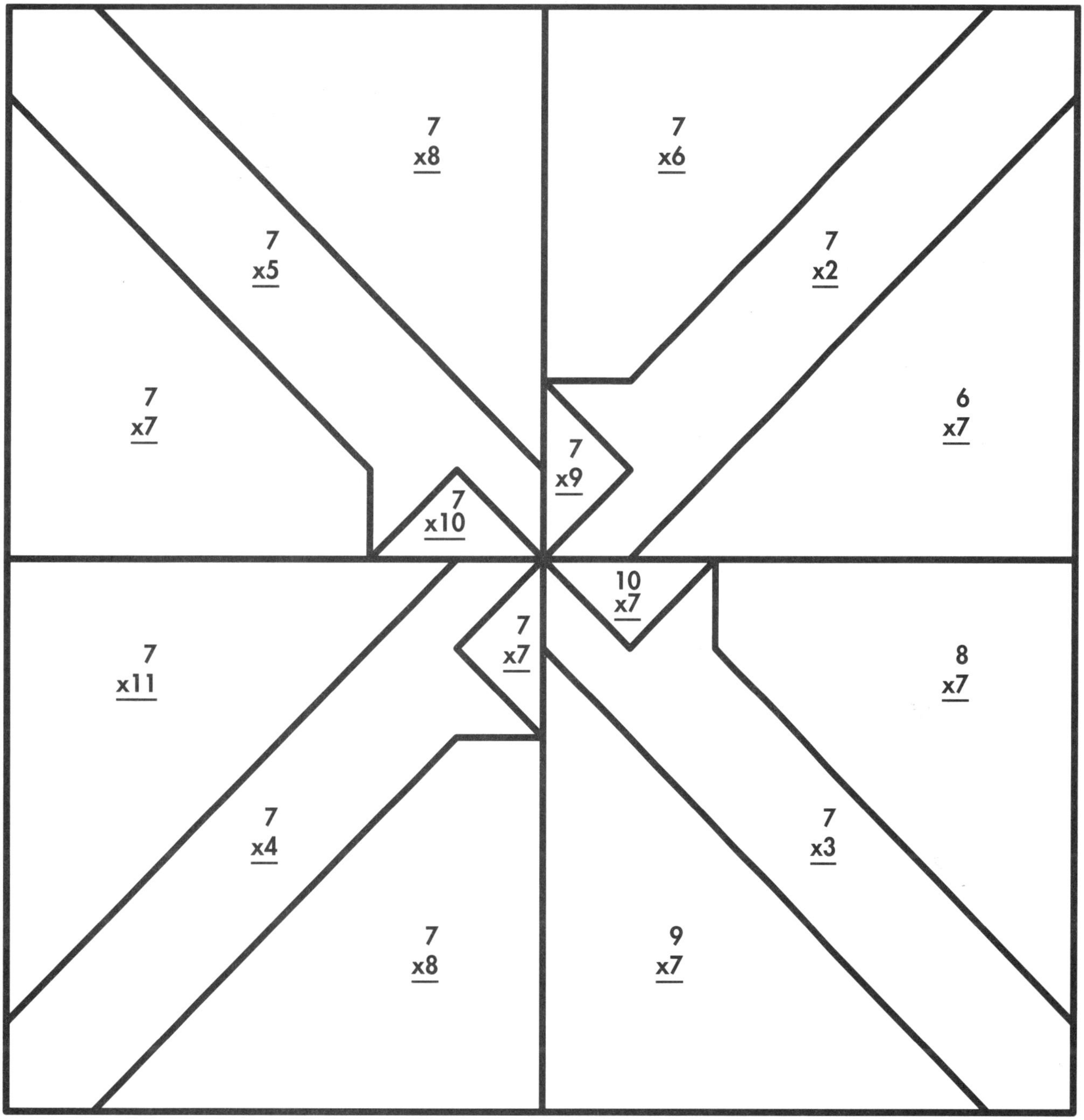

7 x8	7 x6
7 x5	7 x2
7 x7	6 x7
7 x10	7 x9
10 x7	7 x7
7 x11	8 x7
7 x4	7 x3
7 x8	9 x7

Color:

If the answer is less than 40, color the space red.

If the answer is greater than 40, color the space black.

No one knows for sure who Mrs. Morgan was. Some people think she worked to pass a law to allow women to vote.

***C* Make flash cards for the multiplication facts for seven. Practice with a friend.**

Tulip-Tree Leaves

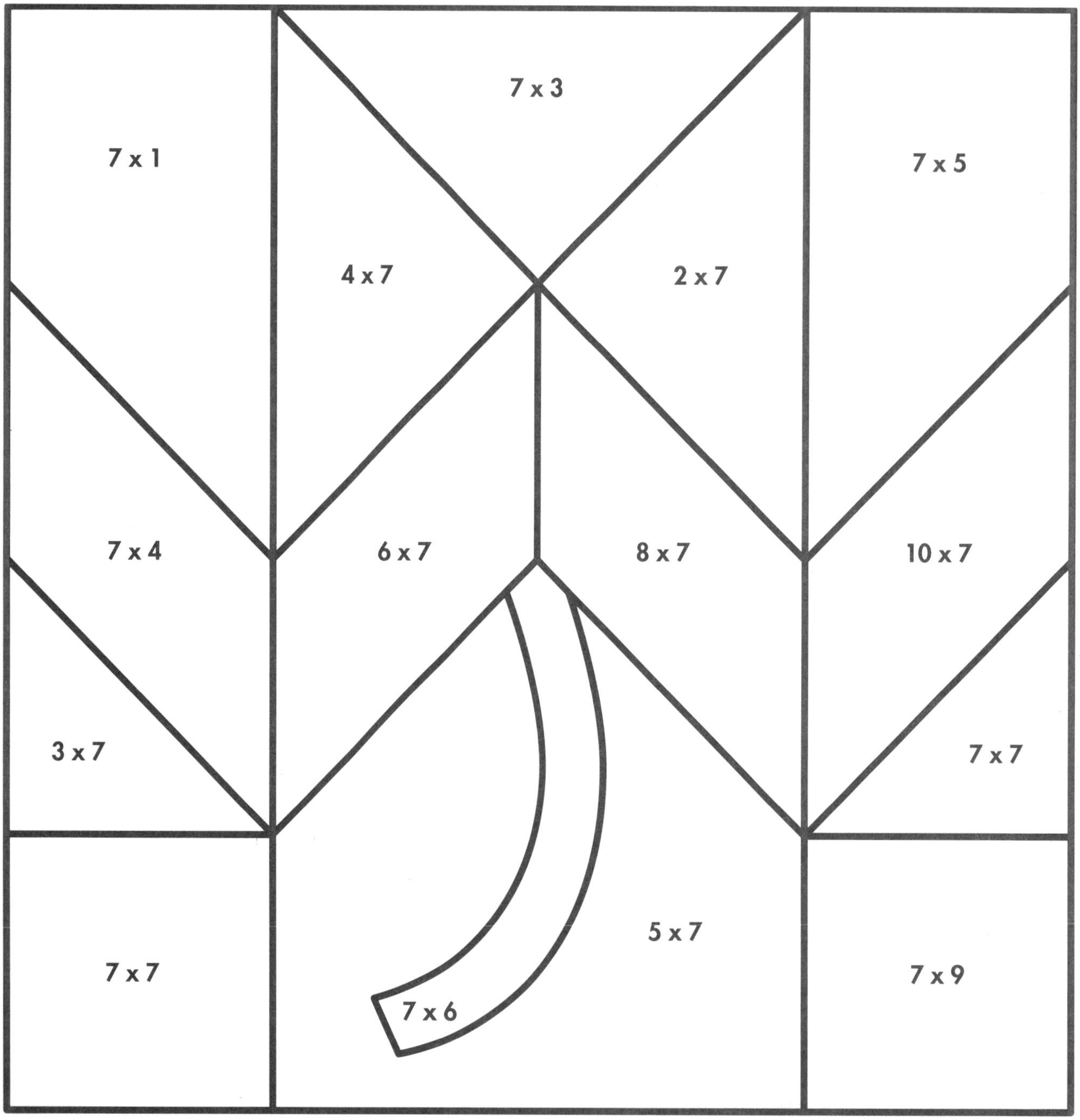

7 x 3

7 x 1

7 x 5

4 x 7

2 x 7

7 x 4

6 x 7

8 x 7

10 x 7

3 x 7

7 x 7

5 x 7

7 x 7

7 x 9

7 x 6

Color:

If the answer is an even number, color the space green.

If the answer is an odd number, color the space yellow.

Trees and leaves are often part of quilt designs. Tulip trees have unusual leaves.

***C* Write the answers to the problems on this page in number order.**

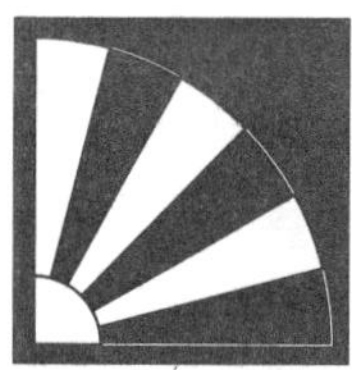

Fannie's Fan

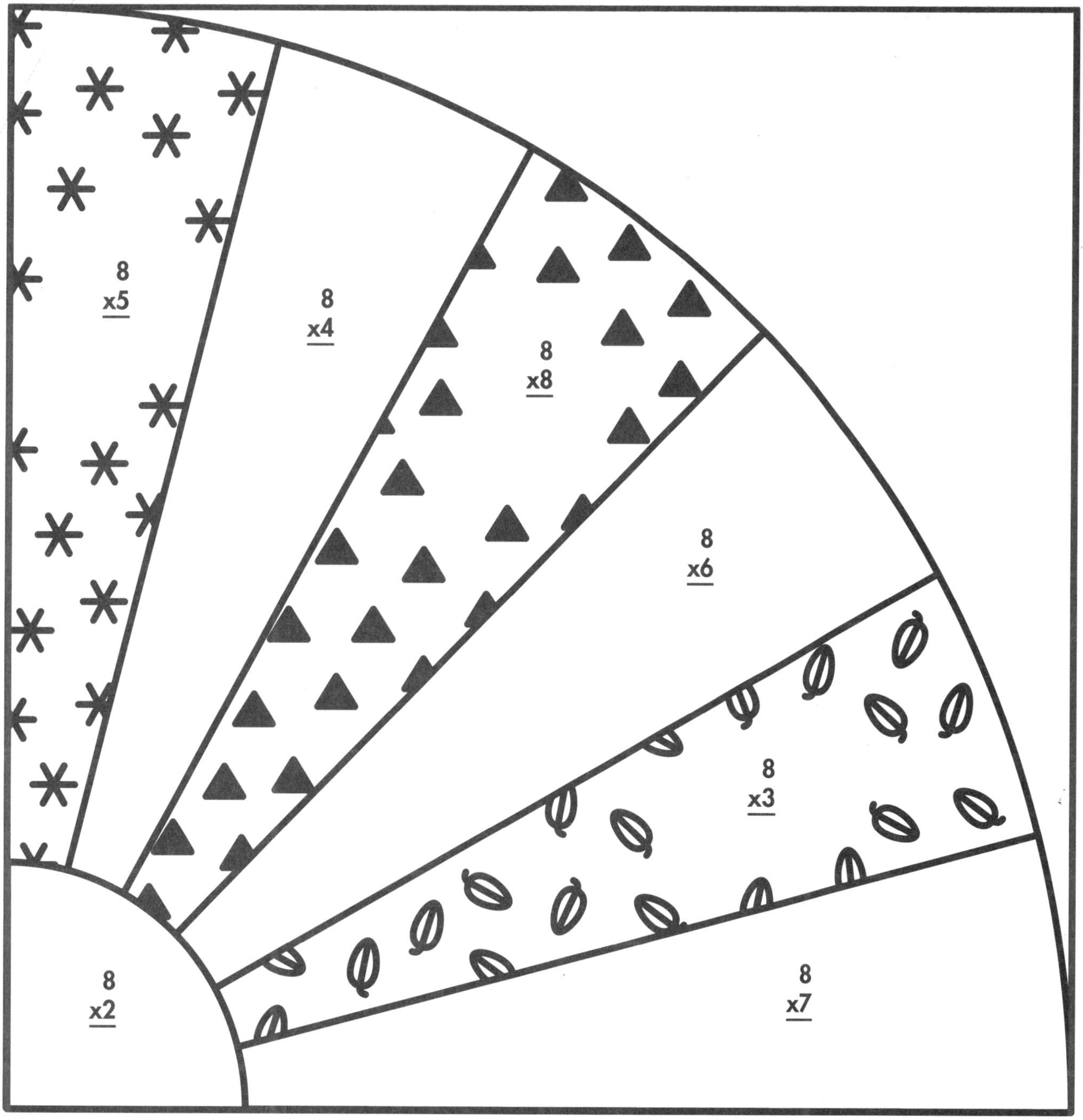

8
x5

8
x4

8
x8

8
x6

8
x3

8
x2

8
x7

Color:

16 = brown
24 = yellow
32 = green
40 = red
48= blue
56= purple
64= orange

In the1800s, quilt makers designed fancy patterns. Fan quilts were very popular.

C **Write the multiplication facts for eight on the back of this sheet of paper.**

54-40 or Fight

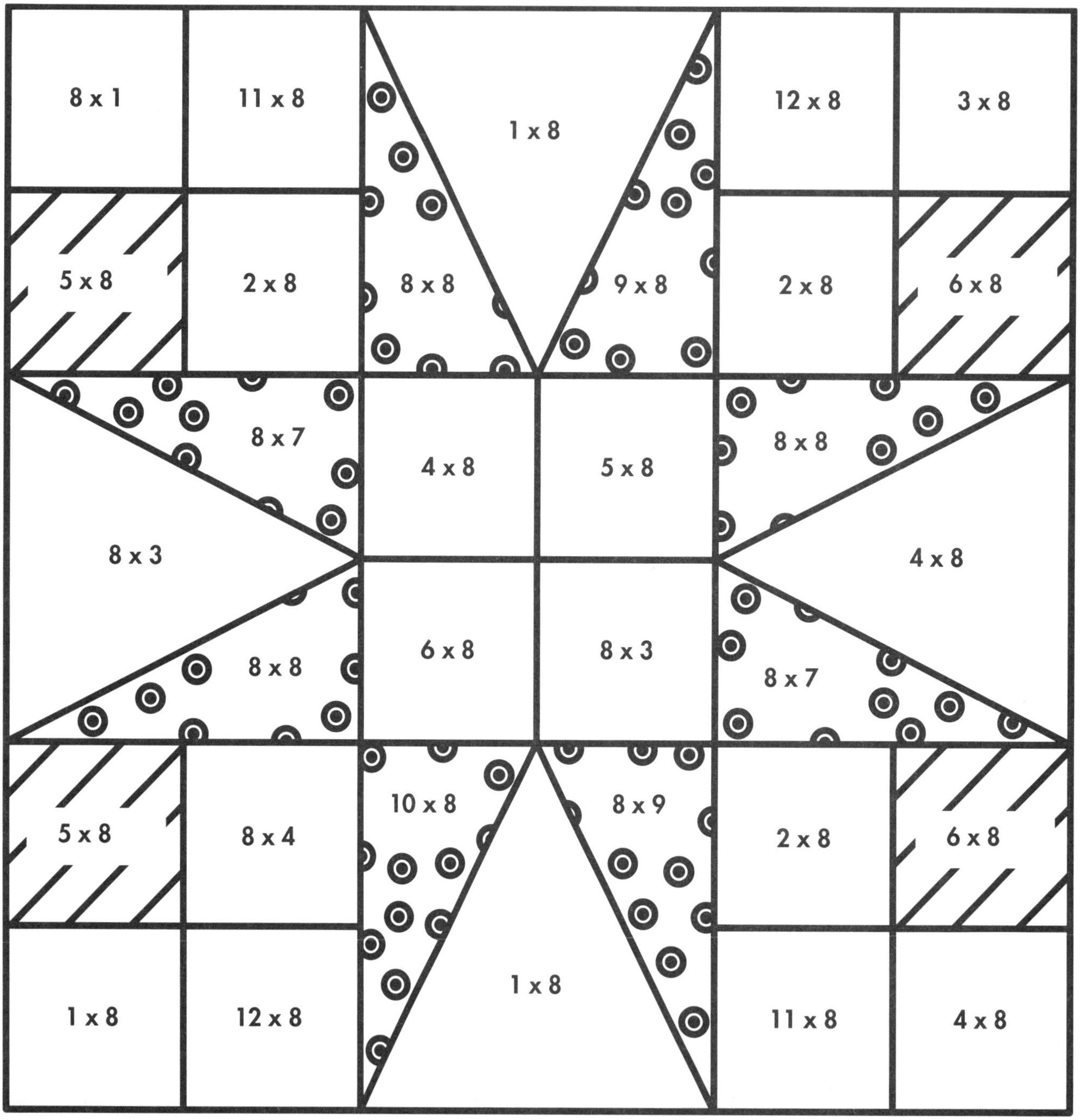

8 x 1
11 x 8
1 x 8
12 x 8
3 x 8
5 x 8
2 x 8
8 x 8
9 x 8
2 x 8
6 x 8
8 x 7
4 x 8
5 x 8
8 x 8
8 x 3
4 x 8
8 x 8
6 x 8
8 x 3
8 x 7
10 x 8
8 x 9
5 x 8
8 x 4
2 x 8
6 x 8
1 x 8
1 x 8
12 x 8
11 x 8
4 x 8

Color:
8, 16, 24, and 32 = orange
56, 64, 72, and 80 = green
40 and 48 = brown
88 and 96 = white

In 1846, the United States and Canada divided up the Northwest Territory. This design represents the new land.

***C* Make a graph showing the number of times each answer appears on this page.**

Kaleidoscope

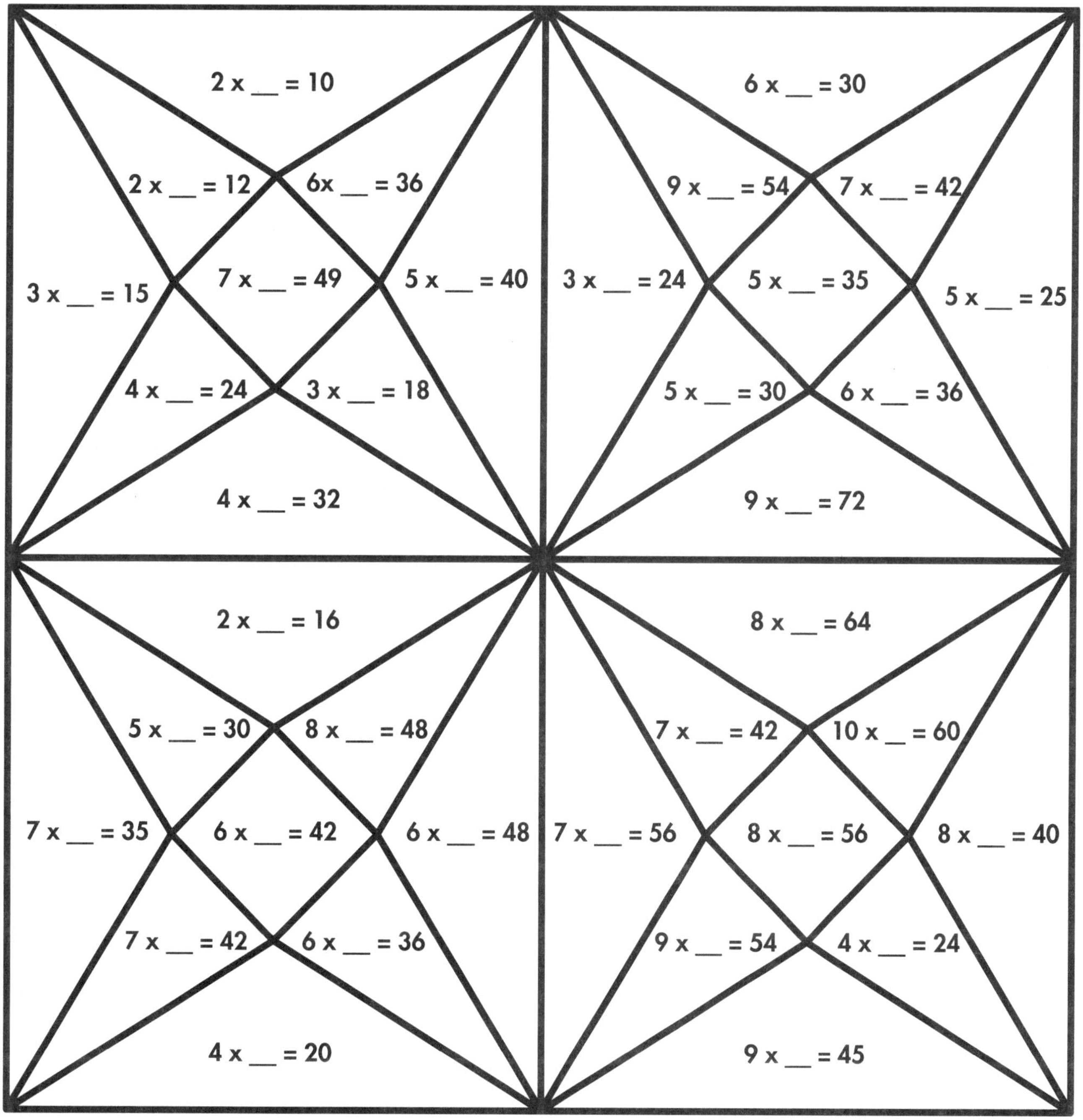

2 x __ = 10

2 x __ = 12

6x __ = 36

3 x __ = 15

7 x __ = 49

5 x __ = 40

4 x __ = 24

3 x __ = 18

4 x __ = 32

6 x __ = 30

9 x __ = 54

7 x __ = 42

3 x __ = 24

5 x __ = 35

5 x __ = 25

5 x __ = 30

6 x __ = 36

9 x __ = 72

2 x __ = 16

5 x __ = 30

8 x __ = 48

7 x __ = 35

6 x __ = 42

6 x __ = 48

7 x __ = 42

6 x __ = 36

4 x __ = 20

8 x __ = 64

7 x __ = 42

10 x __ = 60

7 x __ = 56

8 x __ = 56

8 x __ = 40

9 x __ = 54

4 x __ = 24

9 x __ = 45

Color:

Put in the missing number to complete the problems.

5 = brown

6 = yellow

7 = green

8 = orange

This pattern was designed to look like the popular children's toy. Bits of colored glass form pictures at the end of a long tube when that end is turned.

C **On the back of this sheet of paper, multiply your age by five, six, seven, and eight.**

Spool

10 x 5 | 11 x 6 | 6 x 6

6 x3 | 7 x7 | 3 x7 | 8 x3 | 7 x10 | 6 x3 | 3 x7 | 6 x 7 | 4 x8

6 x9 | 8 x9 | 5 x9

1 x5 | 10 x 6 | 11 x 7

7 x3 | 8 x1 | 3 x8 | 3 x7 | 11 x 5 | 5 x5 | 4 x7 | 12 x 7 | 6 x3

6 x2 | 7 x9 | 9 x8

8 x6 | 5 x3 | 6 x9

6 x4 | 7 x5 | 4 x7 | 4 x8 | 8 x2 | 7 x3 | 6 x4 | 9 x7 | 5 x5

5 x8 | 2 x6 | 12 x 5

Color:
- If the answer is from 0 to 17, color the space green.
- If the answer is from 18 to 32, color the space black.
- If the answer is from 33 to 48, color the space yellow.
- If the answer is from 49 to 64, color the space red.
- If the answer is from 65 to 85, color the space blue.

Many old beds and chairs have legs shaped like spools. This pattern shows what the leg bottoms looked like.

***C* Find a library book about pioneers. Look for pictures of furniture that has spool-shaped legs.**

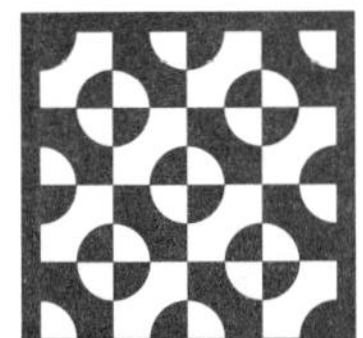

Steeplechase

9 x3	2 x1		3 x2	11 x 5	8 x7		6 x2
	7 x5	7 x2	11 x 3		7 x7	3 x4	3 x7
	4 x3	9 x1	6 x8		5 x2	5 x9	4 x4
4 x7	5 x5		7 x3	8 x4	3 x3		9 x7
3 x5	7 x6	5 x3	6 x3	5 x5	9 x8	3 x3	6 x5
	3 x9	3 x8			7 x11	2 x7	
	4 x5	11 x 3	10 x 8	7 x5	9 x4	5 x5	8 x8
8 x5	9 x3		5 x7	8 x2			9 x3

Color:

If the answer is odd, color the space blue.

If the answer is even, color the space white.

The steeplechase is a horse-riding competition. Horses jump over fences and ponds.

C Counting by threes, write the numbers from three to seventy-eight.

Pine Burr

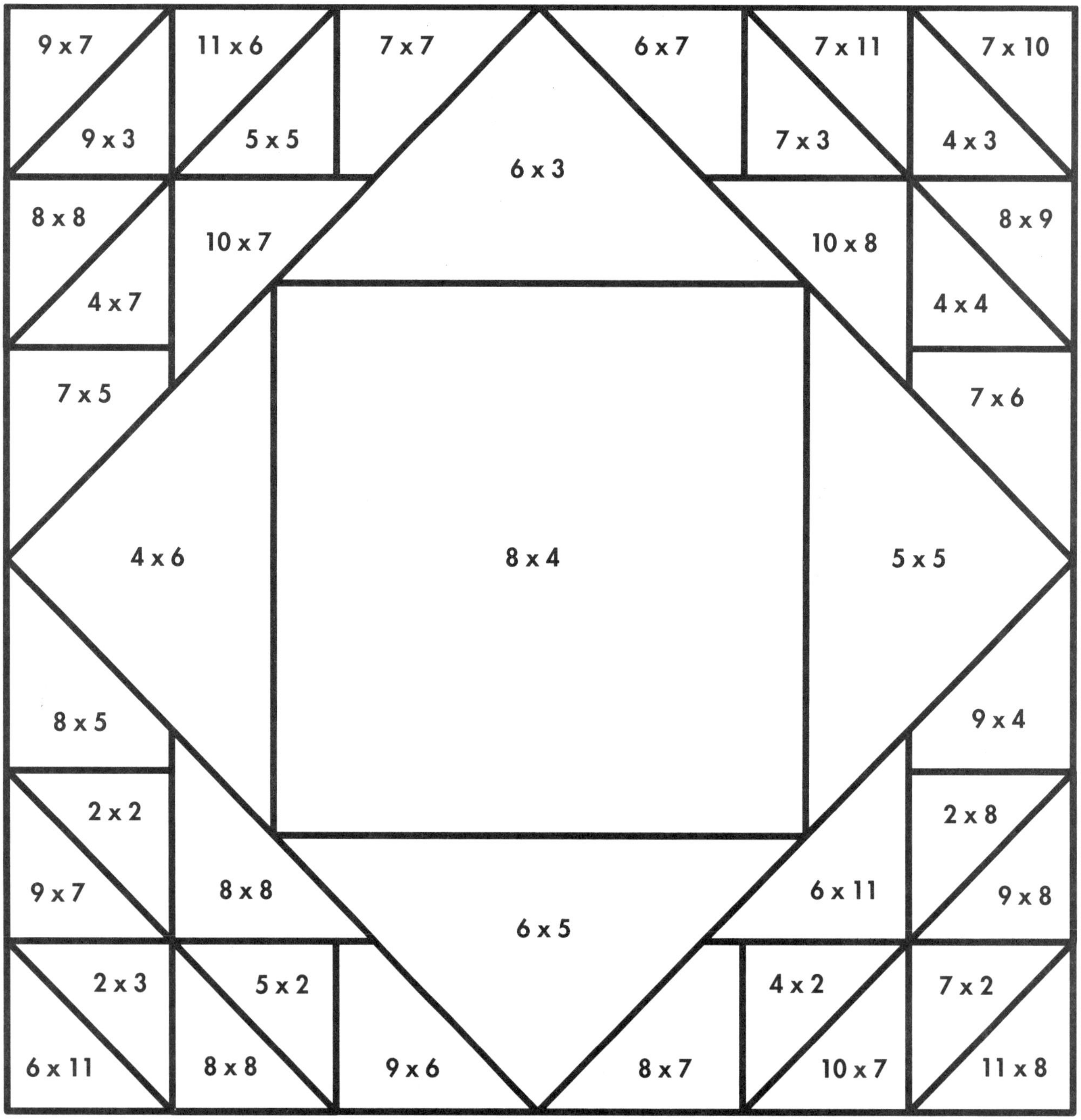

9 x 7
9 x 3
11 x 6
5 x 5
7 x 7
6 x 7
6 x 3
7 x 11
7 x 3
7 x 10
4 x 3
8 x 8
4 x 7
10 x 7
10 x 8
8 x 9
4 x 4
7 x 5
7 x 6
4 x 6
8 x 4
5 x 5
8 x 5
9 x 4
2 x 2
9 x 7
8 x 8
6 x 5
6 x 11
2 x 8
9 x 8
2 x 3
6 x 11
5 x 2
8 x 8
9 x 6
8 x 7
4 x 2
10 x 7
7 x 2
11 x 8

Color:

If the answer is from 0 to 30, color the space green.

If the answer is from 31 to 60, color the space yellow.

If the answer is from 61 to 90, color the space red.

Pioneers found pine trees on almost all the land they explored. Part of this design has a pinecone shape.

***C* Circle fifteen answers on this page. Write them in number order.**

String of Beads

9 x1		2 x9

9 x5 — 8 x9 — 9 x6

9 x9 — 9 x11

9 x8 — 9 x7

10 x 9 — 11 x 9

9 x 4 — 7 x 9 — 5 x 9

9 x 2 — 9 x 3

Color:

9, 18, and 27 = blue
63 and 72 = green
36, 45, and 54 = yellow
81, 90, and 99 = red

In pioneer days, people made their own beads out of wood or glass. Then they strung them into necklaces.

***C* On the back of this sheet of paper, draw a picture of a decoration you have made.**

Beggar Block

9 x 7

9 x 5 | 1 x 9 | 9 x 6 | 9 x 2 | 9 x 9 | 9 x 3 | 9 x 10

9 x 8

9 x 11 | 10 x 9

9 x 4 | 2 x 9

7 x 9 | 9 x 9

9 x 8

6 x 9 | 9 x 1 | 5 x 9 | 4 x 9 | 7 x 9 | 3 x 9 | 8 x 9

6 x 9

Color:

If the answer is from 9 to 36, color the space yellow.

If the answer is from 45 to 99, color the space red.

This pattern name refers to the custom of "begging" for quilt scraps from friends and neighbors.

***C* On the back of this sheet of paper, multiply your age by nine.**

Snow on the Mountain

10
x 5

10
x 1

10
x 7

10
x 8

10
x 9

10
x 4

10
x 2

10
x 10

10
x 4

10
x 3

30

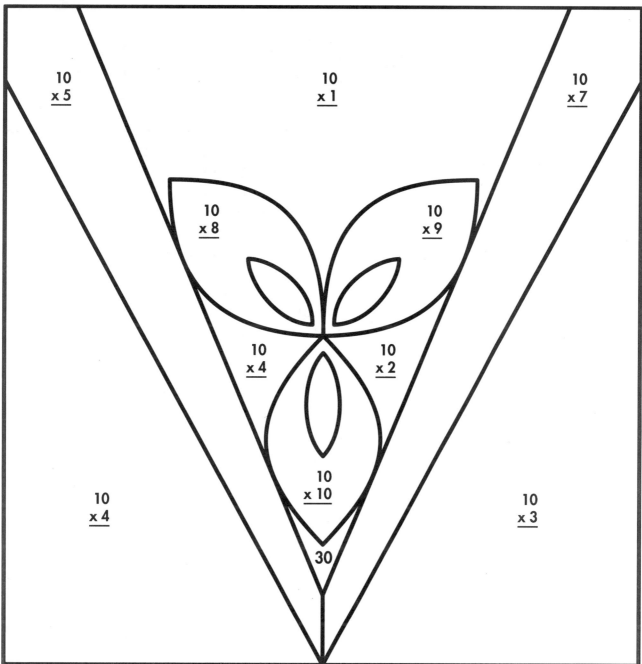

Color:
If the answer is from
10 to 40, color the space brown.
If the answer is from
50 to 70, color the space green.
If the answer is from
80 to 100, color the space blue.

When you solve the color code for this pattern, you may see why it has its name.

C Find a picture of a snow-covered mountain.

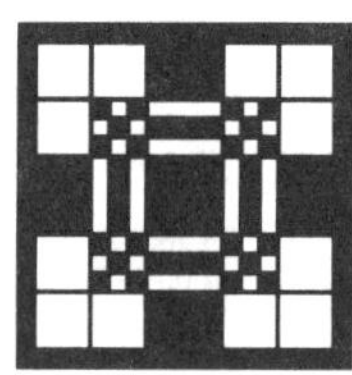

Album Patch

10 x 5	10 x 1			7 x 10	1 x 10			6 x 10
10 x 2	90		80	10 x 4	90		80	2 x 10
		100		10 x 9		90		
	80		90	10 x 3	80		80	
10 x 7	3 x10	10 x8	4 x10	Sign name here	2 x10	10 x10	1 x10	7 x 10
10 x 3	80		90	3 x 10	80		90	4 x 10
		100		9 x 10		80		
	90		80	4 x 10	90		80	
10 x 6	10 x 4			5 x 10	3 x 10			6 x 10

Color:

10, 20, 30, and 40 = red
50, 60, and 70 = green
80, 90, and 100 = blue

The Album Patch quilt was usually made for one person by a group of her friends. Each friend made a square and signed her name in the middle.

***C* After this page is completed, sign your name on the line. Then tape several squares together to form an album quilt.**

Double Tulip

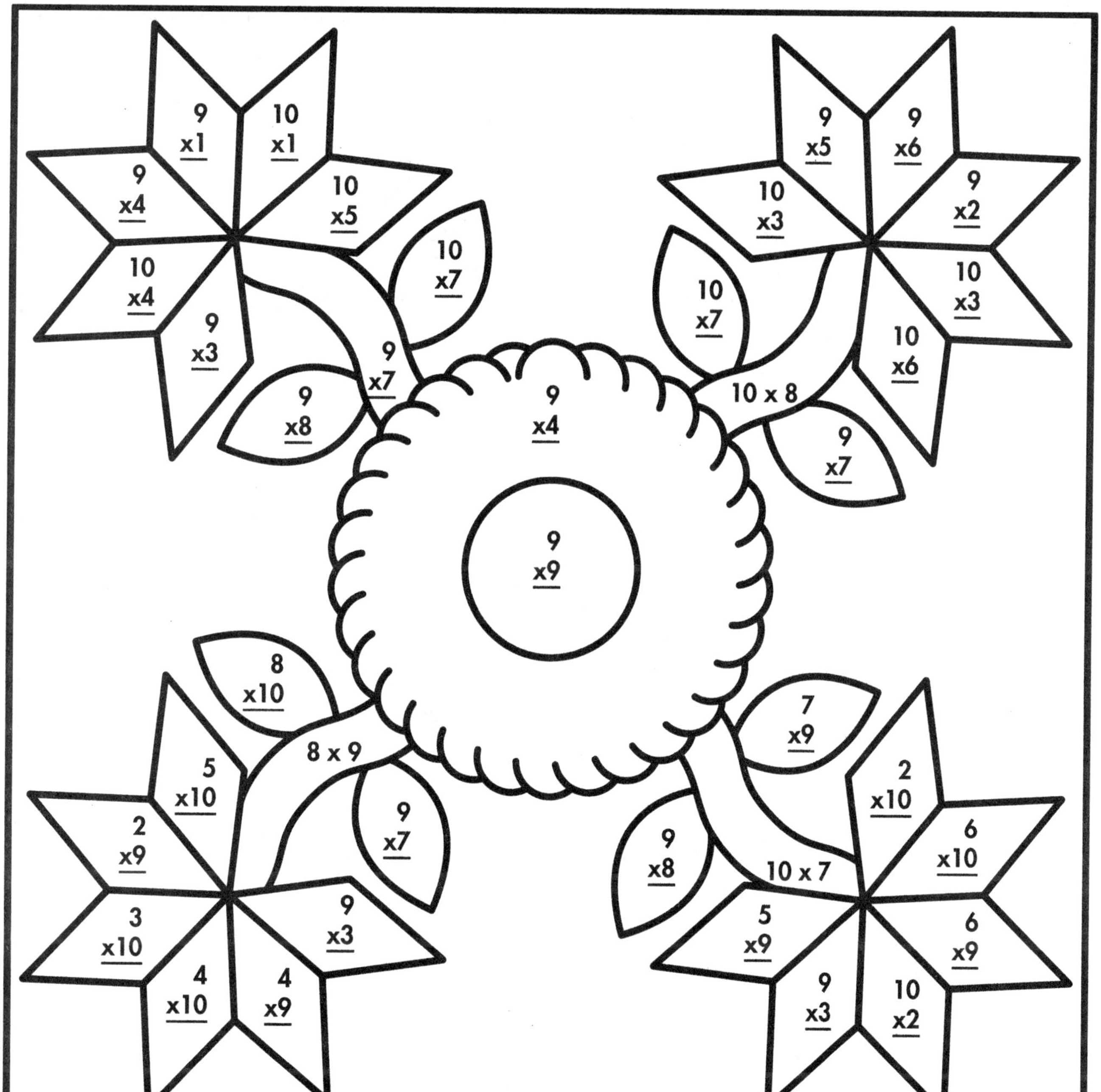

Color:

If the answer is from 9 to 30, color the space orange.
If the answer is from 36 to 60, color the space red.
If the answer is from 63 to 80, color the space green.
If the answer is from 81 to 100, color the space yellow.

In midwestern states, this pattern is named for the tulip. In other parts of the country, people call it Double Lily.

***C* Find pictures or draw pictures of a tulip and a lily. How are the flowers the same? How are they different?**

Spice Pinks

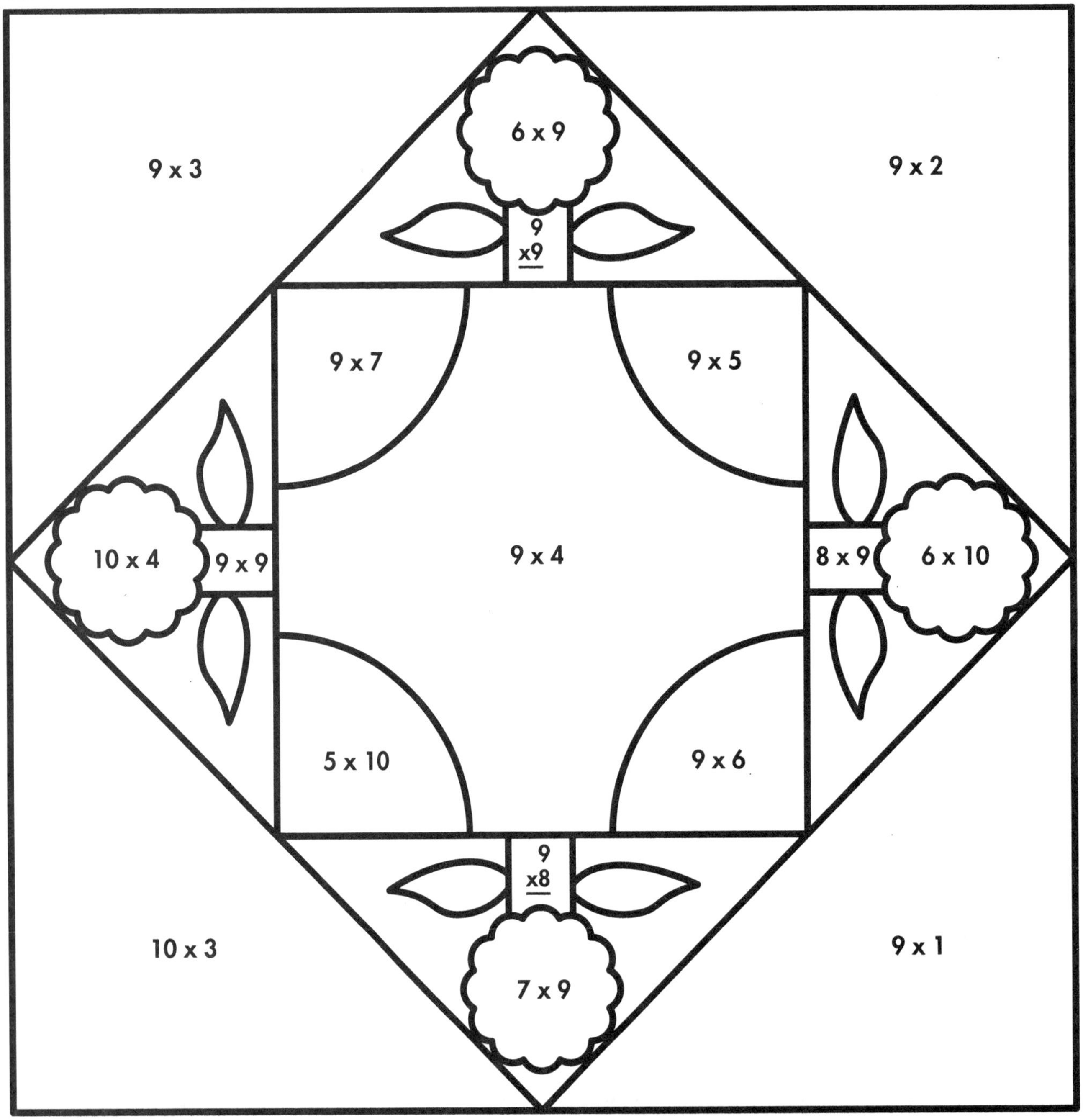

9 x 3

6 x 9

9 x 2

9
x9

9 x 7

9 x 5

10 x 4

9 x 9

9 x 4

8 x 9

6 x 10

5 x 10

9 x 6

9
x8

10 x 3

9 x 1

7 x 9

Color:

If the answer is from 9 to 36, color the space blue.

If the answer is from 40 to 63, color the space pink.

If the answer is from 70 to 100, color the space green.

This pattern looks like someone's plan for planting a garden.

***C* On the back of this sheet of paper, write the names of three flowers you like. Then draw a picture of one of the flowers.**

Ice-Cream Cone

9
x4
8
x3
7
x3
7
x4
10 x 9
9 x 6
9 x 8
9 x 9
7 x 6
6
x5
7
x2
6
x3
5
x6
5
x7
10 x 8
8 x 8
7 x 7
10 x 9
8
x4
8
x5
6
x5
6
x6
9 x 10
8 x 9
10 x 8
6 x 8
9 x 7
5
x5
4
x4
3
x4
3
x7
2
x7

Color:

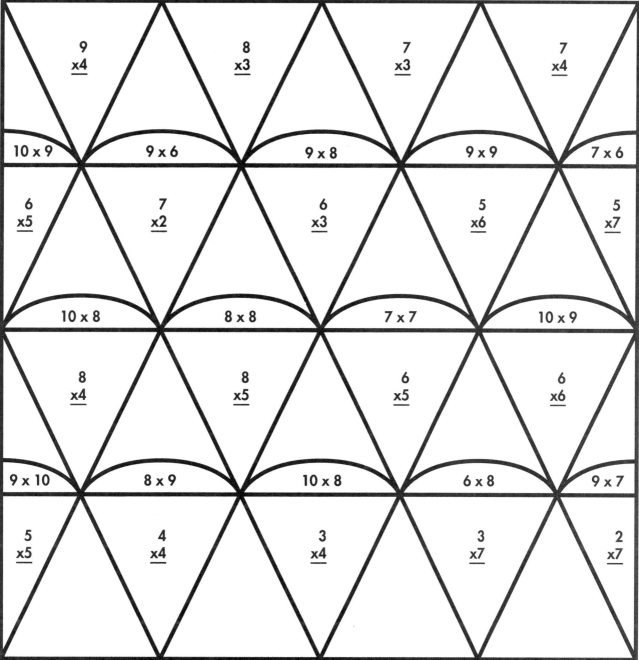

If the answer is from 0 to 40, color the space brown.

If the answer is from 41 to 50, color the space red.

If the answer is from 51 to 70, color the space orange.

If the answer is from 71 to 80, color the space yellow.

If the answer is from 81 to 90, color the space green.

This pattern first appeared in the early 1900s. It was used to advertise National Dairy Week.

***C* Name two special days in this month. Draw a picture to advertise one of the days.**

x1 to x 10

Autograph Patch

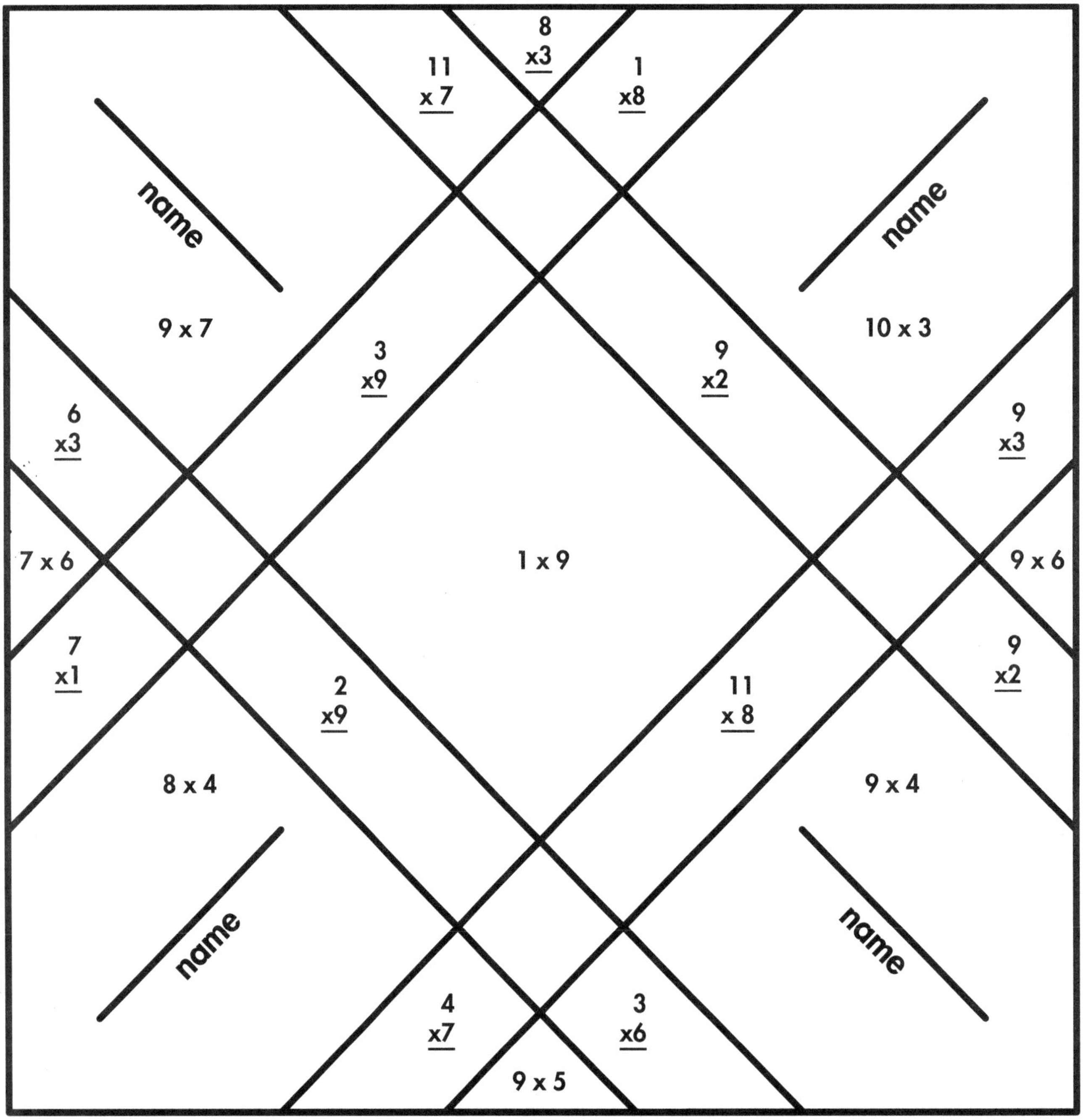

8
x3

11
x 7

1
x8

name

name

9 x 7

3
x9

9
x2

10 x 3

6
x3

9
x3

7 x 6

1 x 9

9 x 6

7
x1

9
x2

2
x9

11
x 8

8 x 4

9 x 4

name

name

4
x7

3
x6

9 x 5

Color:

If the answer has a 3 in it, color the space green.
If the answer has a 4 in it, color the space orange.
If the answer has a 7 or 8 in it, color the space blue.
If the answer has a 9 in it, color the space yellow.

The Autograph Patch was often made by friends who signed their names on the patch. This kind of special quilt was rarely used. It was usually saved as a keepsake.

***C* Describe something that you use to remember friends.**

Two digits x one digit/ no regrouping

Lazy Daisy

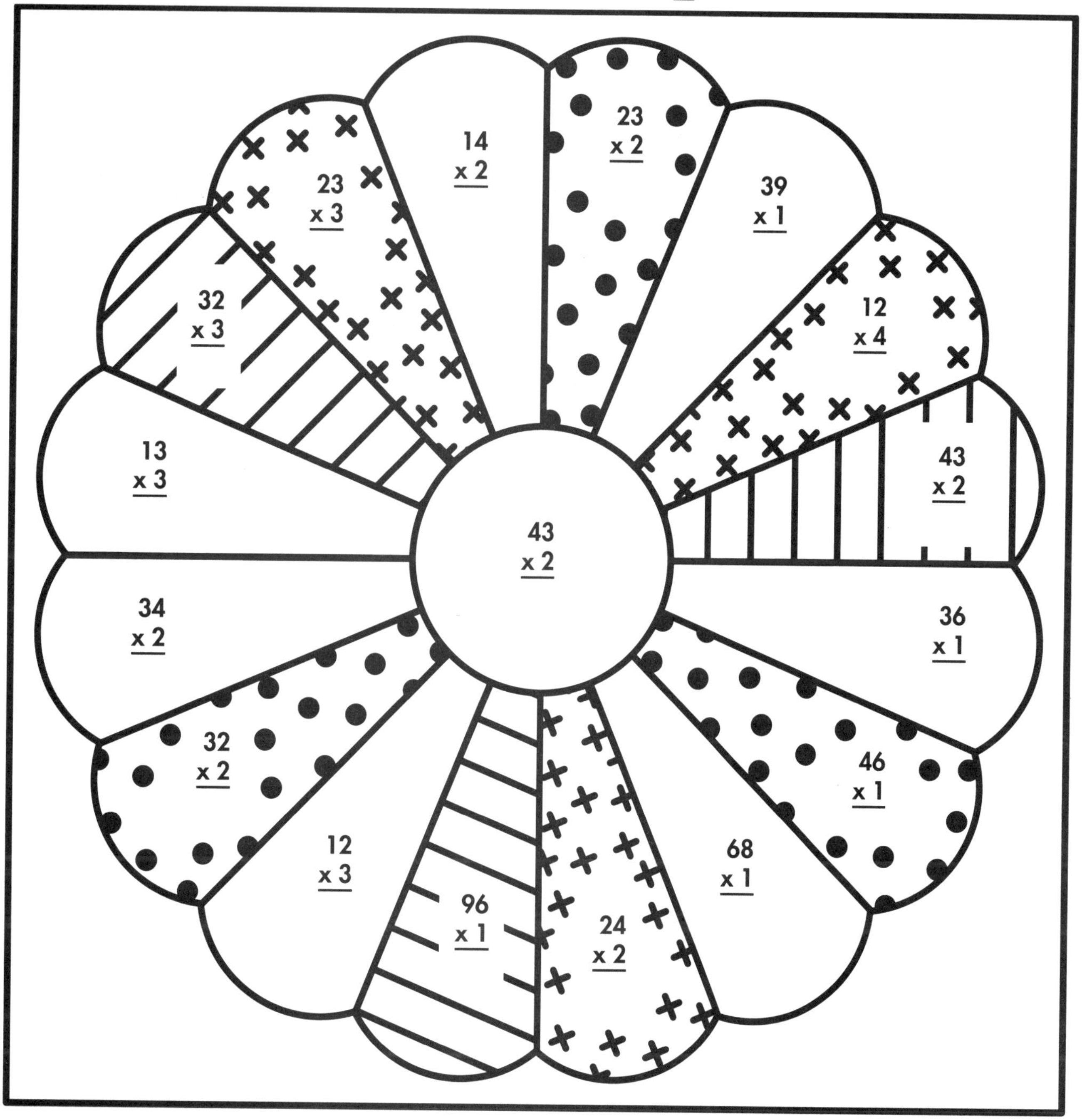

14 x 2	
23 x 2	
23 x 3	
39 x 1	
32 x 3	
12 x 4	
13 x 3	
43 x 2	
43 x 2	
34 x 2	
36 x 1	
32 x 2	
46 x 1	
12 x 3	
68 x 1	
96 x 1	
24 x 2	

Color:

28 and 68 = yellow
36 and 39 = blue
46 and 64 = orange
48 and 69 = green
86 and 96 = red

In pioneer days, daisies grew wild in the fields. Today many people plant them in their gardens.

C Circle the tens place in each answer on this page.

Two digits x one digit/ no regrouping

Poinsettia

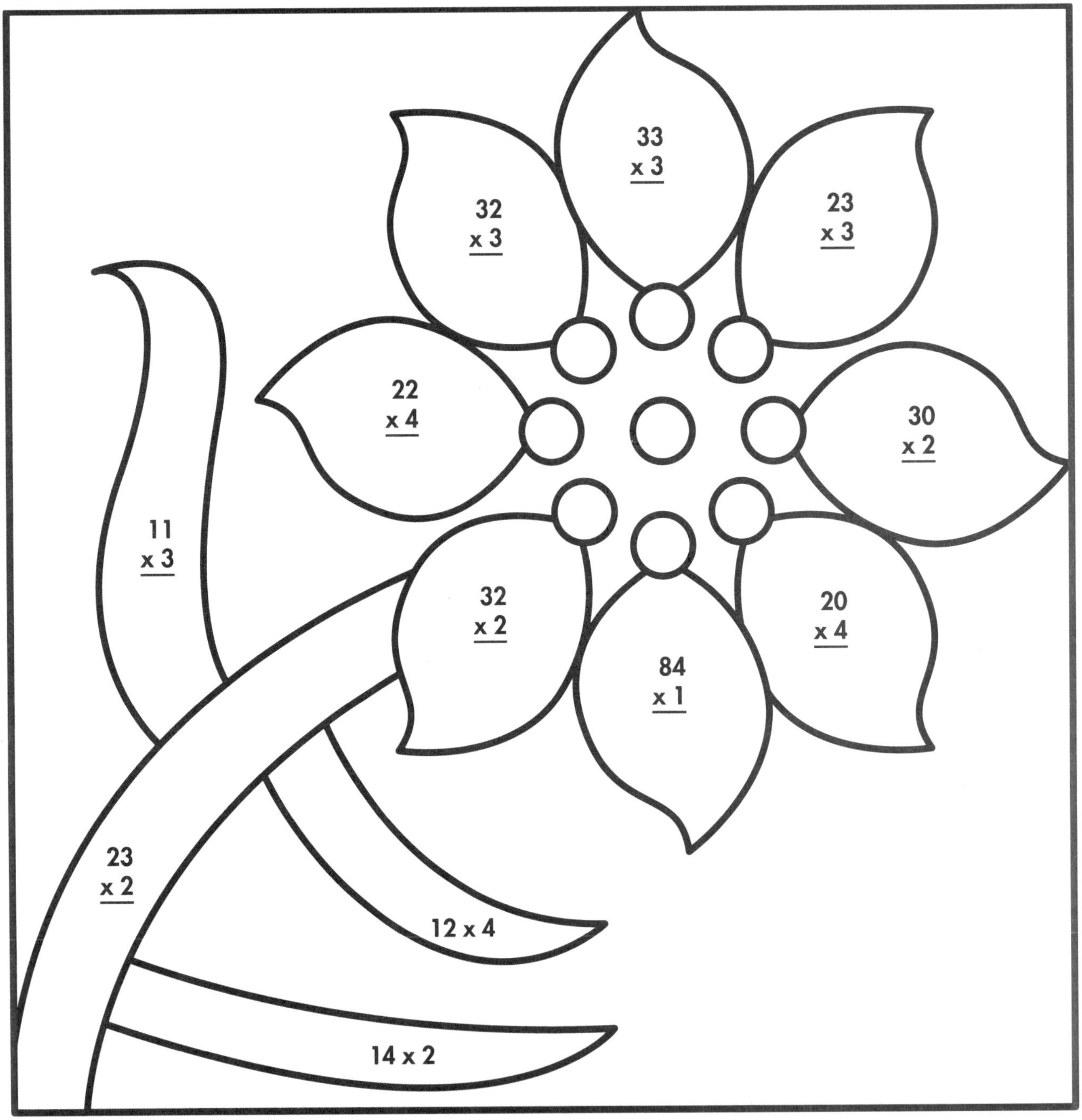

Color:

If the answer is greater than 50, color the space red.

If the answer is less than 50, color the space green.

The poinsettia is a popular Christmas flower.

C Write three problems on the back of this sheet of paper. Model your problems on the ones on this page.

Two digits x one digit/ regroup

Conventional Tulip

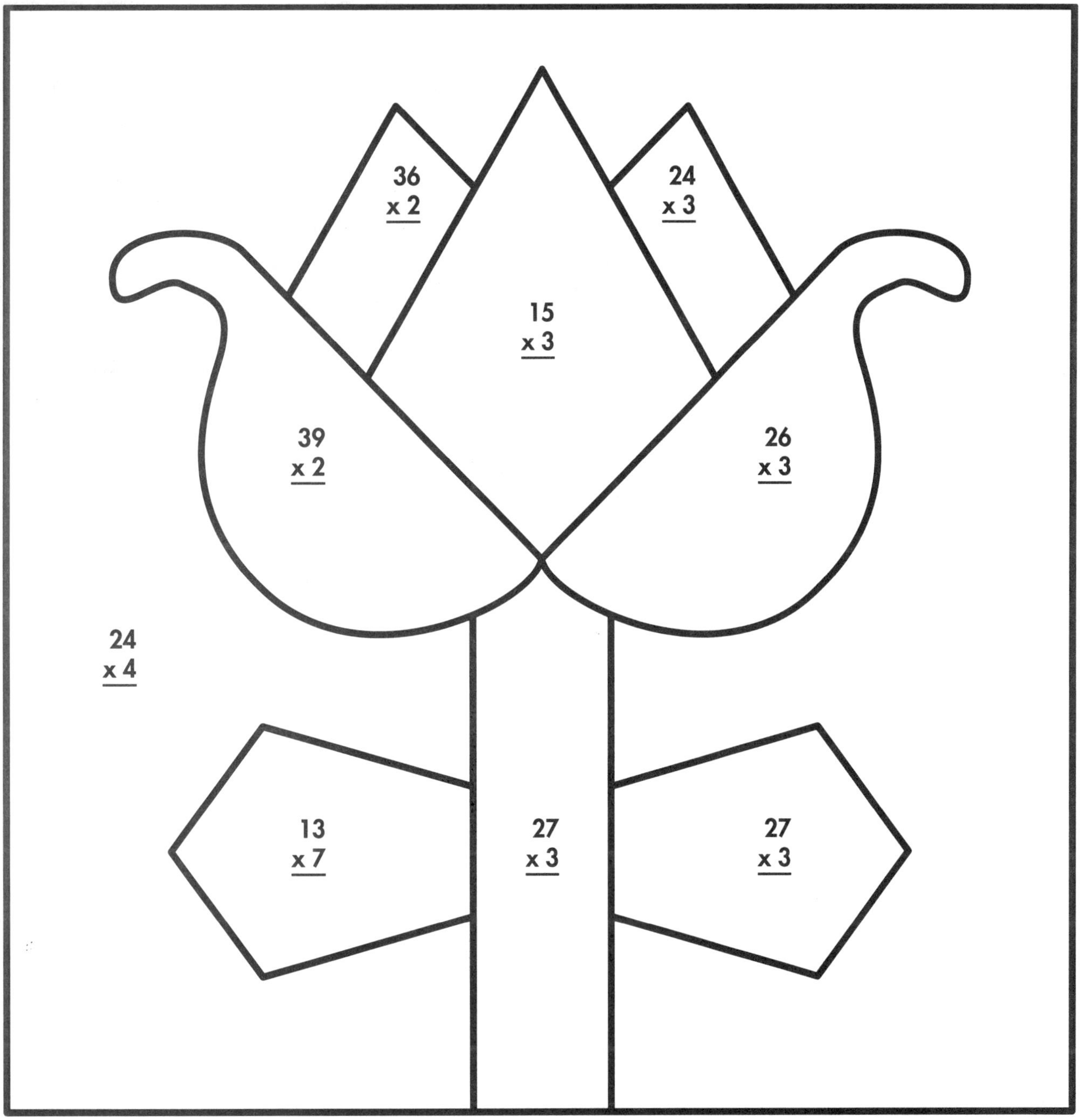

Color:

72 = red
96 = yellow
45 and 78 = orange
81 and 91 = green

This pattern was probably inspired by tulips growing in a garden.

***C* On the back of this sheet of paper, write three problems of your own. Each must use regrouping.**

Two digits x one digit/ regroup

Magnolia Bud

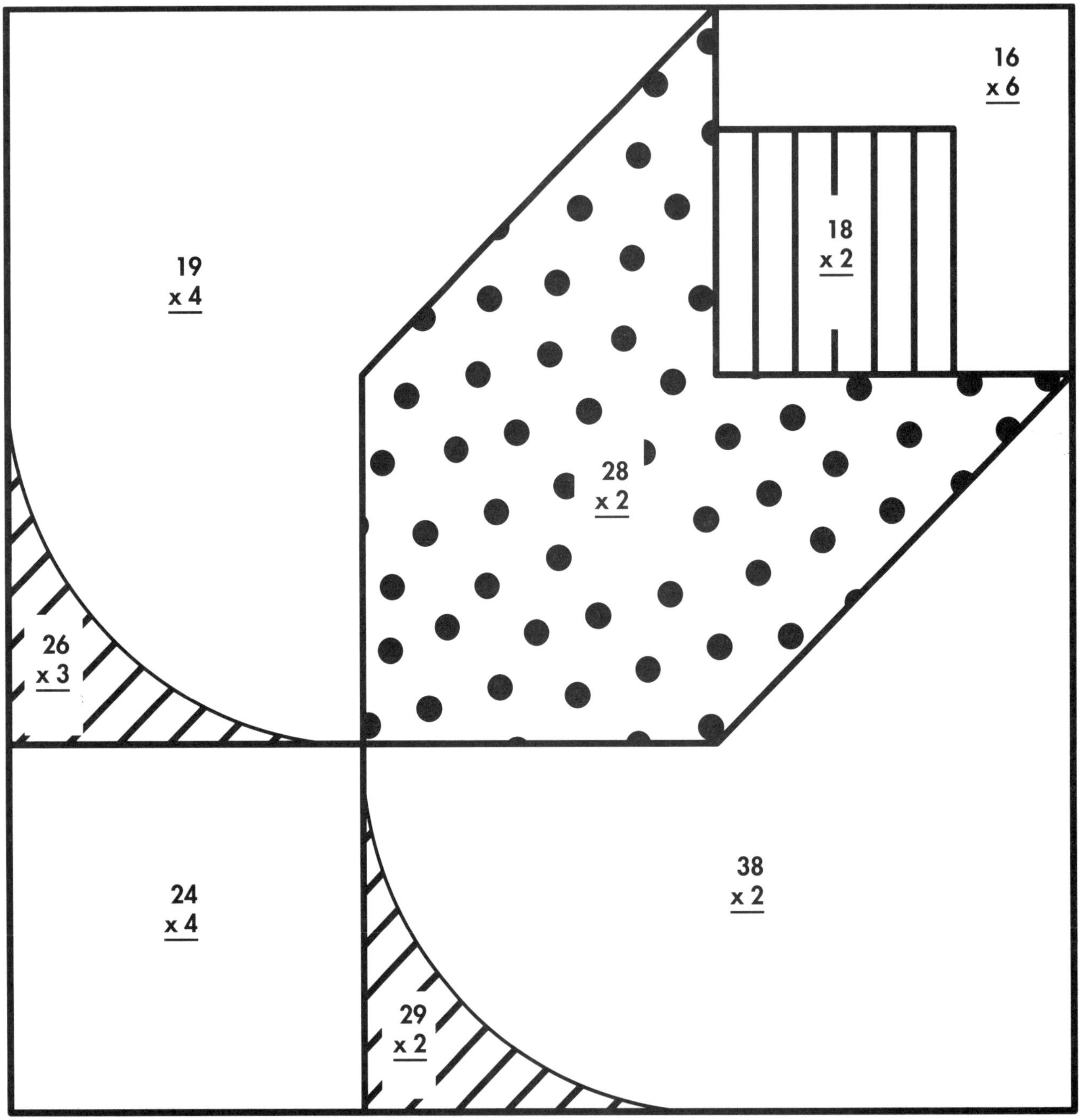

Color:

36 = yellow
56 = orange
76 and 96 = blue
58 and 78 = green

Since the magnolia is a southern tree, this pattern was probably used mostly by southern quiltmakers.

***C* On the back of this sheet of paper, write the names of three trees that grow in your part of the country.**

Queen Charlotte's Crown

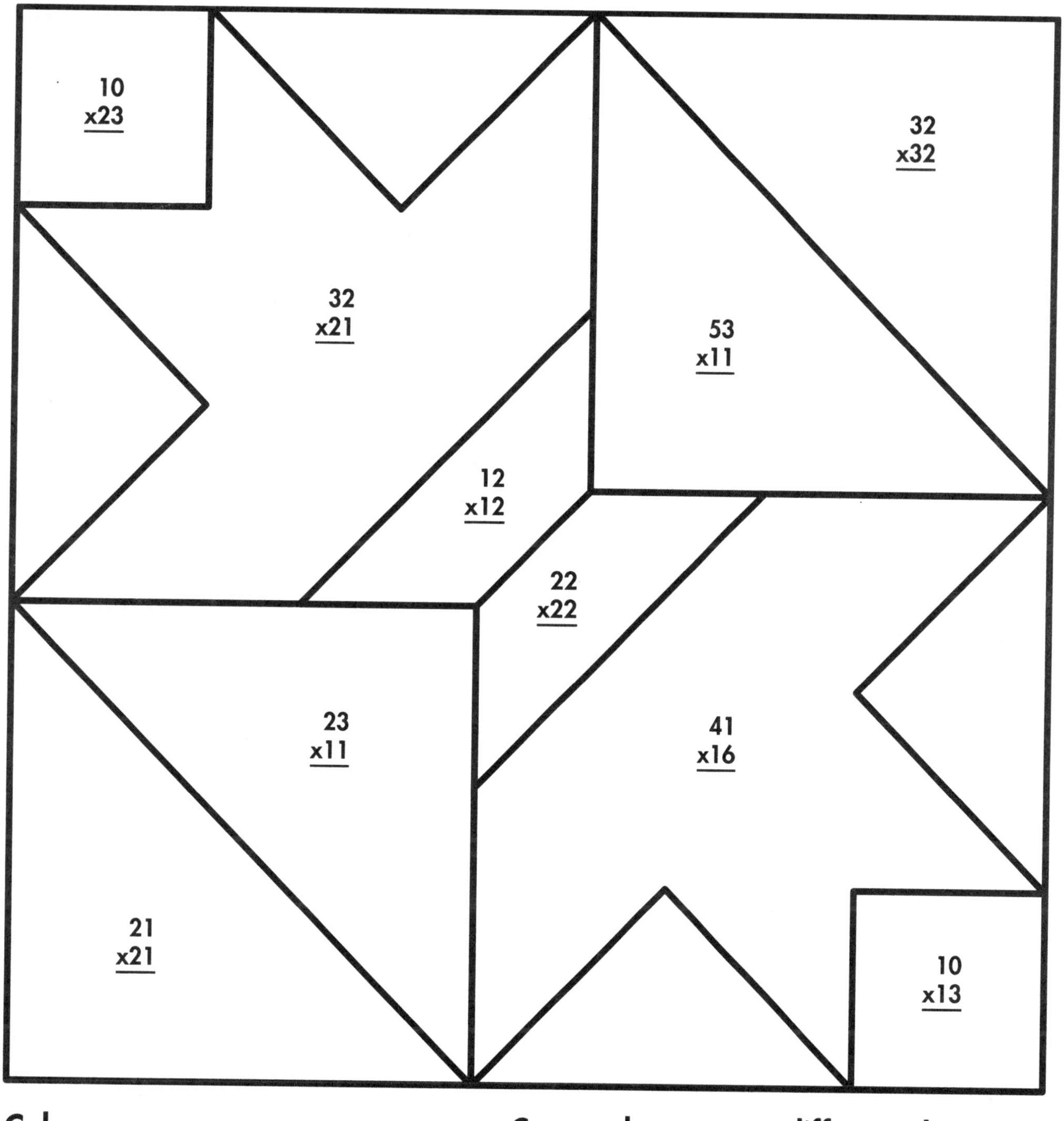

10
x23

32
x32

32
x21

53
x11

12
x12

22
x22

23
x11

41
x16

21
x21

10
x13

Color:

If the answer has a 3 in it, color the space red.
If the answer has a 4 in it, color the space yellow.
If the answer has a 6 in it, color the space brown.

Crowns have many different shapes. This pattern is designed for a crown with a very tall front.

C On the back of this sheet of paper, write the answers on this page in number order.

Snail's Trail

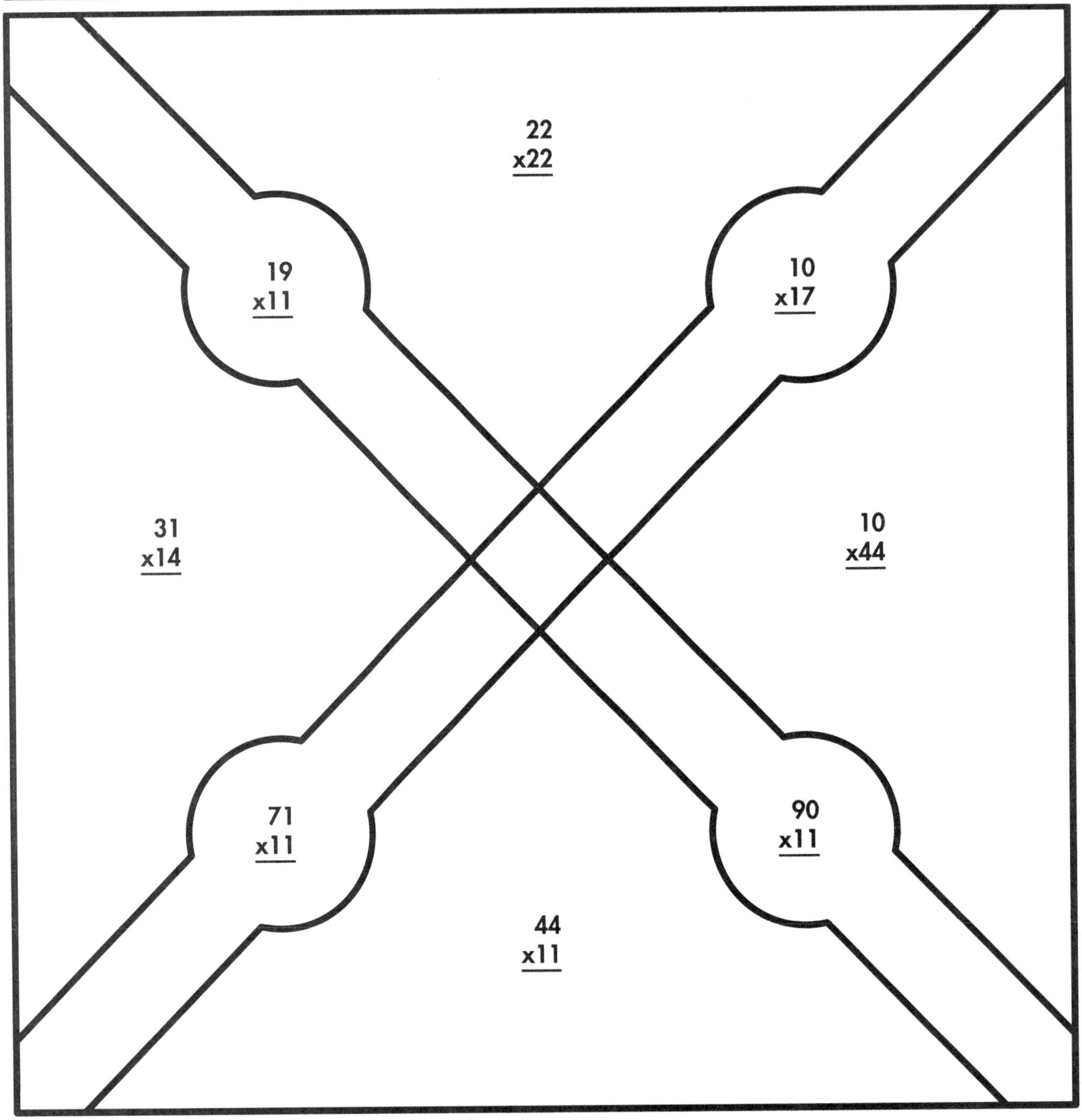

Two digits x two digits/ no regrouping

22
x22

19
x11

10
x17

31
x14

10
x44

71
x11

90
x11

44
x11

Color:

If the answer has a 4 in it, color the space green.

If the answer has a 7 in it, color the space brown.

If the answer has a 9 in it, color the space black.

Snails travel very slowly and leave long, thin trails.

C Circle the tens place and box the ones place in each answer on this page.

Wonder of the World

39 x23	39 x21	21 x14	34 x14
26 x36	18 x18	25 x40	24 x12
32 x13	23 x30	42 x23	44 x14
56 x17	27 x13	16 x32	24 x23

Color:

If the answer is from 100 to 300, color the space red.
If the answer is from 301 to 500, color the space brown.
If the answer is from 501 to 700, color the space blue.
If the answer is from 700 to 1000, color the space green.

People don't know where this quilt name came from. What shapes do you see in the design? What do they make you think of?

____

***C* Select two numbers from 45 to 99. Multiply each by 24.**

Moon Over the Mountain

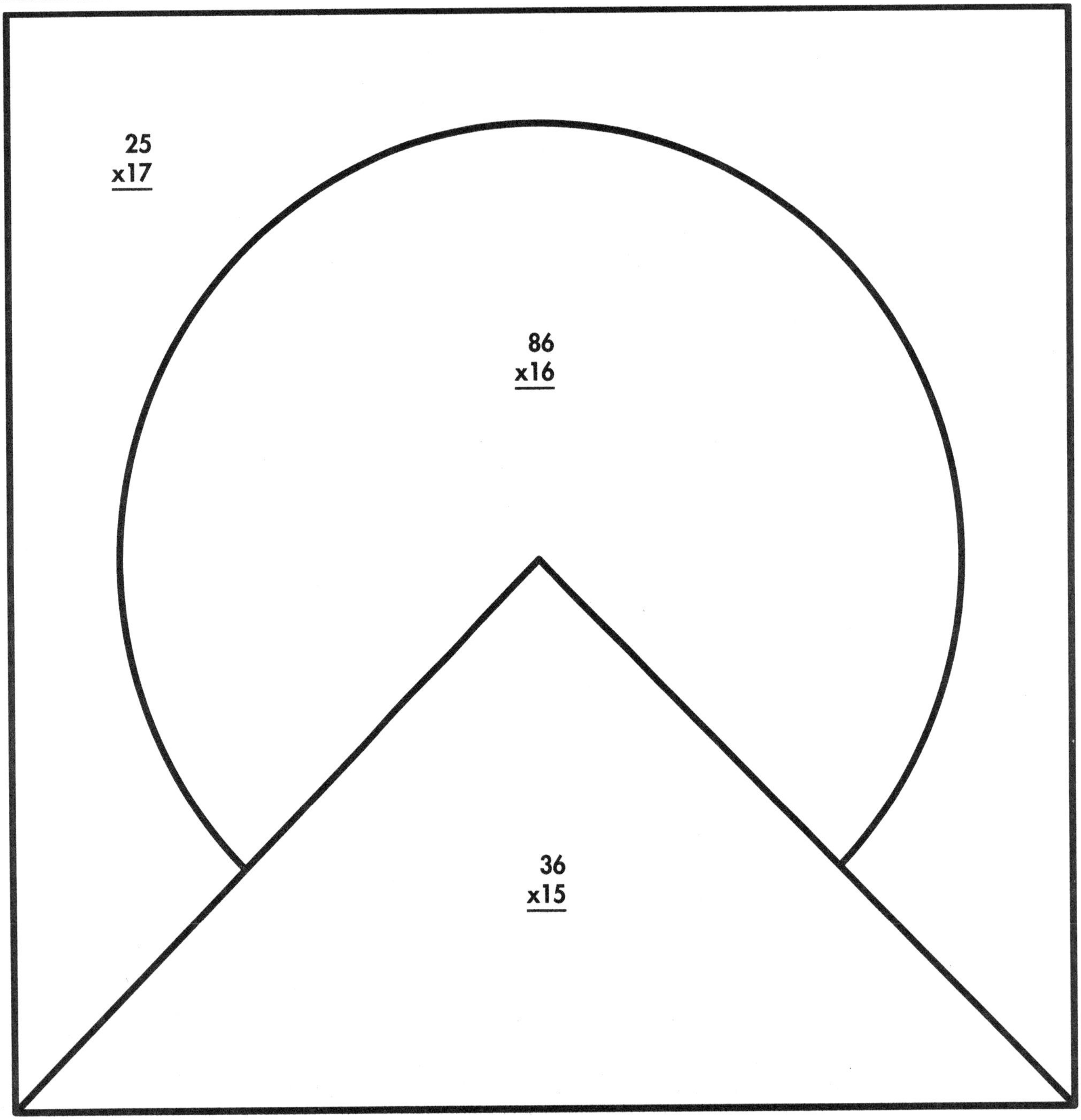

25
x17

86
x16

36
x15

Color:

425 = blue
540 = brown
1376 = yellow

Scenes in nature have always been popular for quilt designs.

***C* Select two numbers from 34 to 87. Multiply each by 16.**

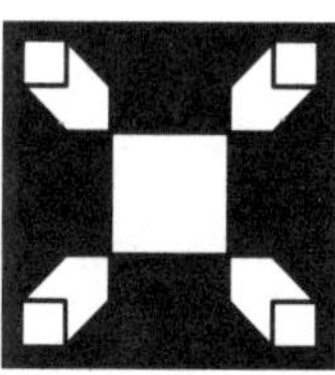

Three digits x one digit/ no regrouping

Tulip Lady Fingers

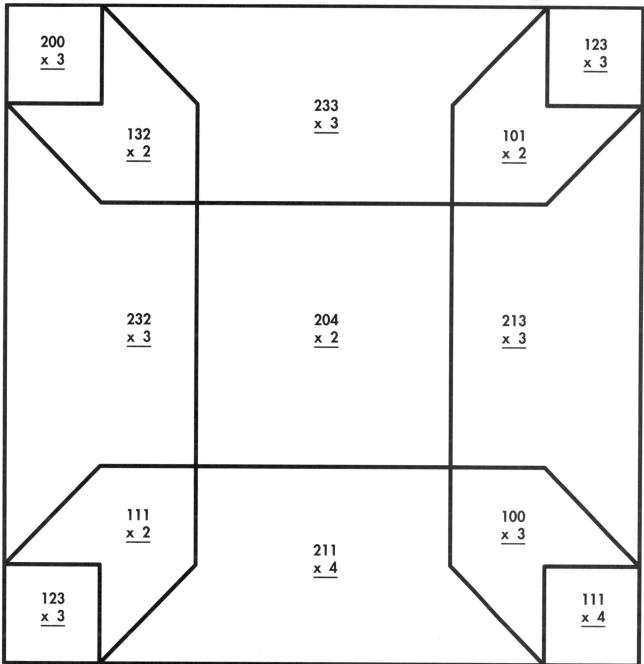

200 x 3	132 x 2	233 x 3	101 x 2	123 x 3
	232 x 3	204 x 2	213 x 3	
123 x 3	111 x 2	211 x 4	100 x 3	111 x 4

Color:

If the answer is from 100 to 300, color the space red.
If the answer is from 301 to 600, color the space green.
If the answer is from 601 to 900, color the space black.

Can you see the tulips in each corner of this pattern?

C Write the names of five kinds of flowers on the back of this sheet of paper.

Three digits x one digit/ no regrouping

Sailboat

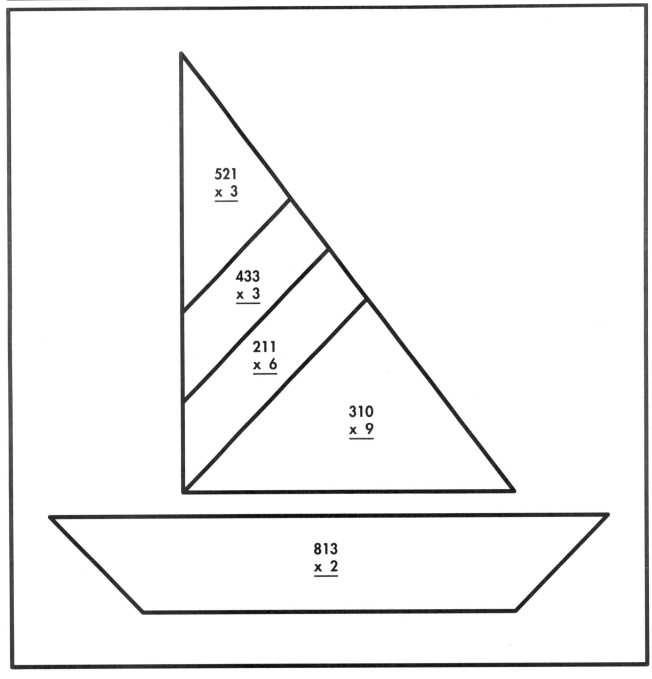

521
x 3

433
x 3

211
x 6

310
x 9

813
x 2

Color:
1266 = red
1299 = yellow
1563 = orange
1626 = black
2790 = green

This is a modern quilt design. Does it look like sailboats you have seen?

***C* Circle the tens place and box the hundreds place in each answer on this page.**

Three digits x two digits/ no regrouping

Amish Diamond

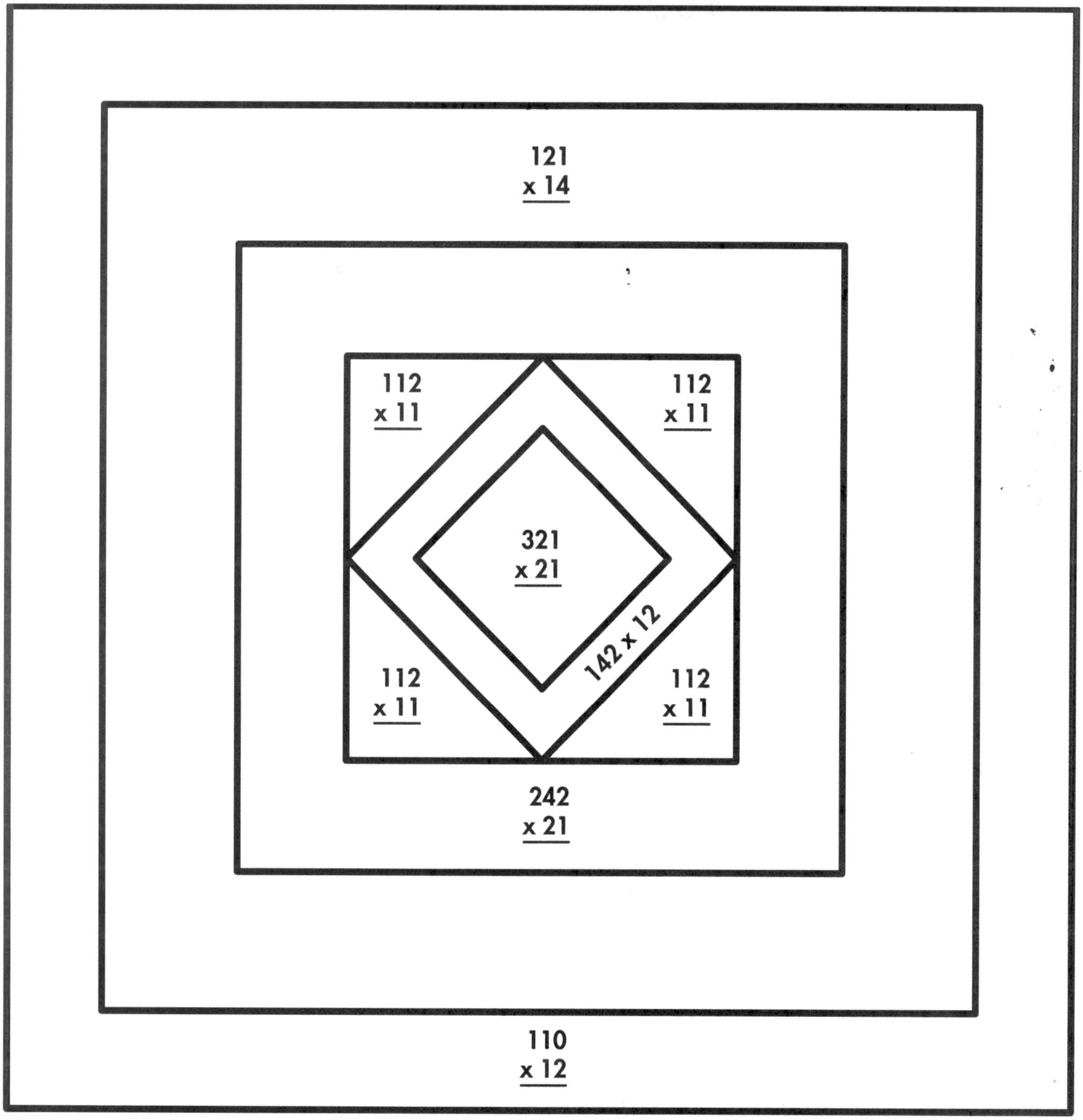

121
x 14

112
x 11

112
x 11

321
x 21

142 x 12

112
x 11

112
x 11

242
x 21

110
x 12

Color:

1232 = blue
1320 and 5082 = purple
1694 and 1704 = red
6741 = pink

This pattern is used in quilts sewn by Amish people.

***C* Find a book about Amish people in the library. List three new facts about Amish people on the back of this sheet of paper.**

Patience Corner

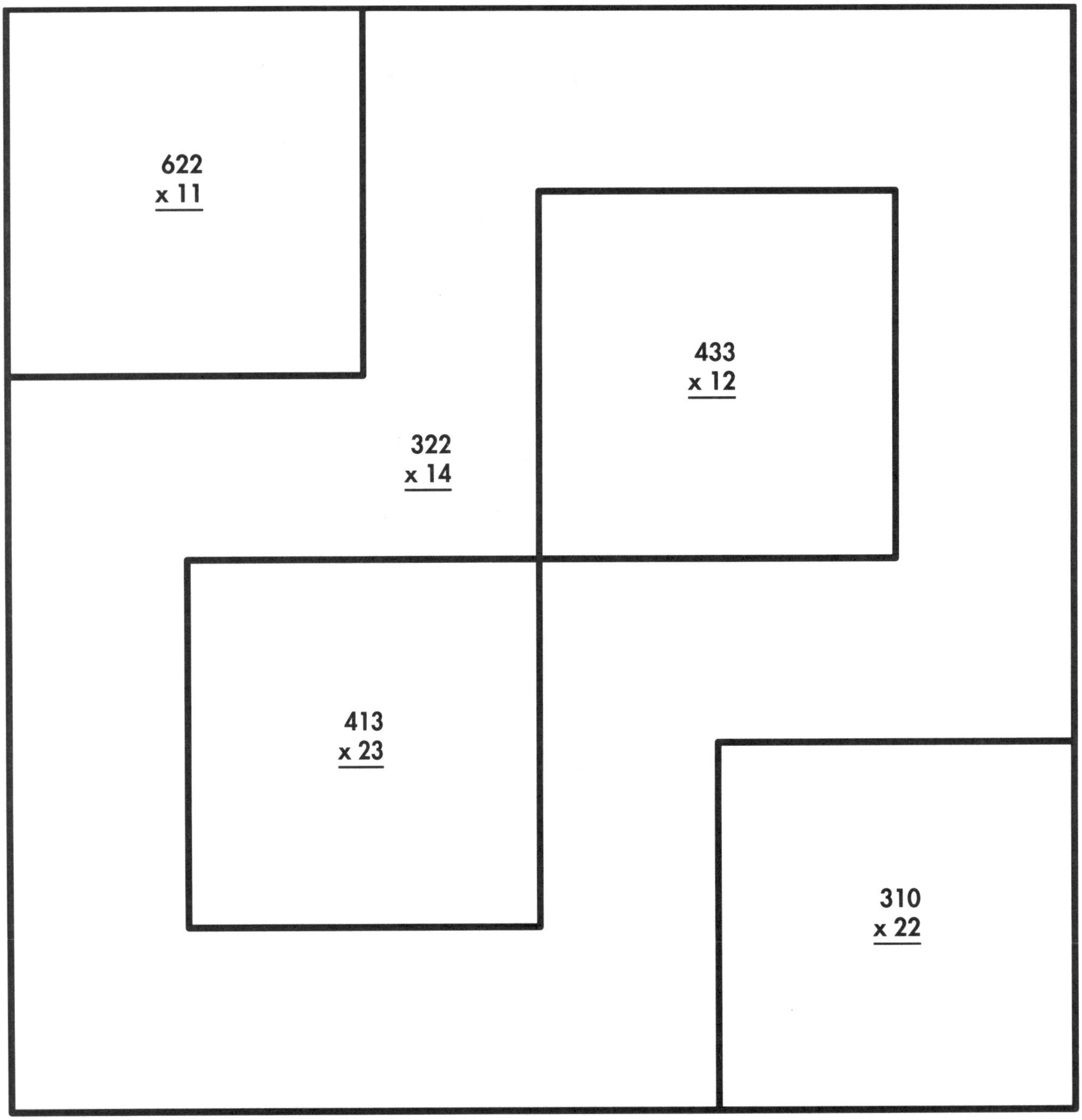

622
x 11

433
x 12

322
x 14

413
x 23

310
x 22

Color:

If the answer is greater than 5000, color the space blue.

If the answer is less than 5000, color the space green.

Long ago, when pupils misbehaved, the teacher asked them to sit in the "patience corner" until they could be good.

***C* Find the dictionary page number for "patience." Multiply that number by 11.**

Checkerboard

213 x 10	648 x 10	326 x 10	213 x 30
326 x 20	436 x 10	435 x 30	435 x 10
247 x 10	638 x 10	319 x 10	213 x 60
122 x 70	265 x 10	249 x 30	132 x 10

Color:

If the answer is less than 5000, color the space red.

If the answer is greater than 5000, color the space black.

This design was named for the popular red and black board game.

***C* Put an X on every box that has a one in the hundreds place.**

Three digits x two digits multiples of 10

Wheel of Fortune

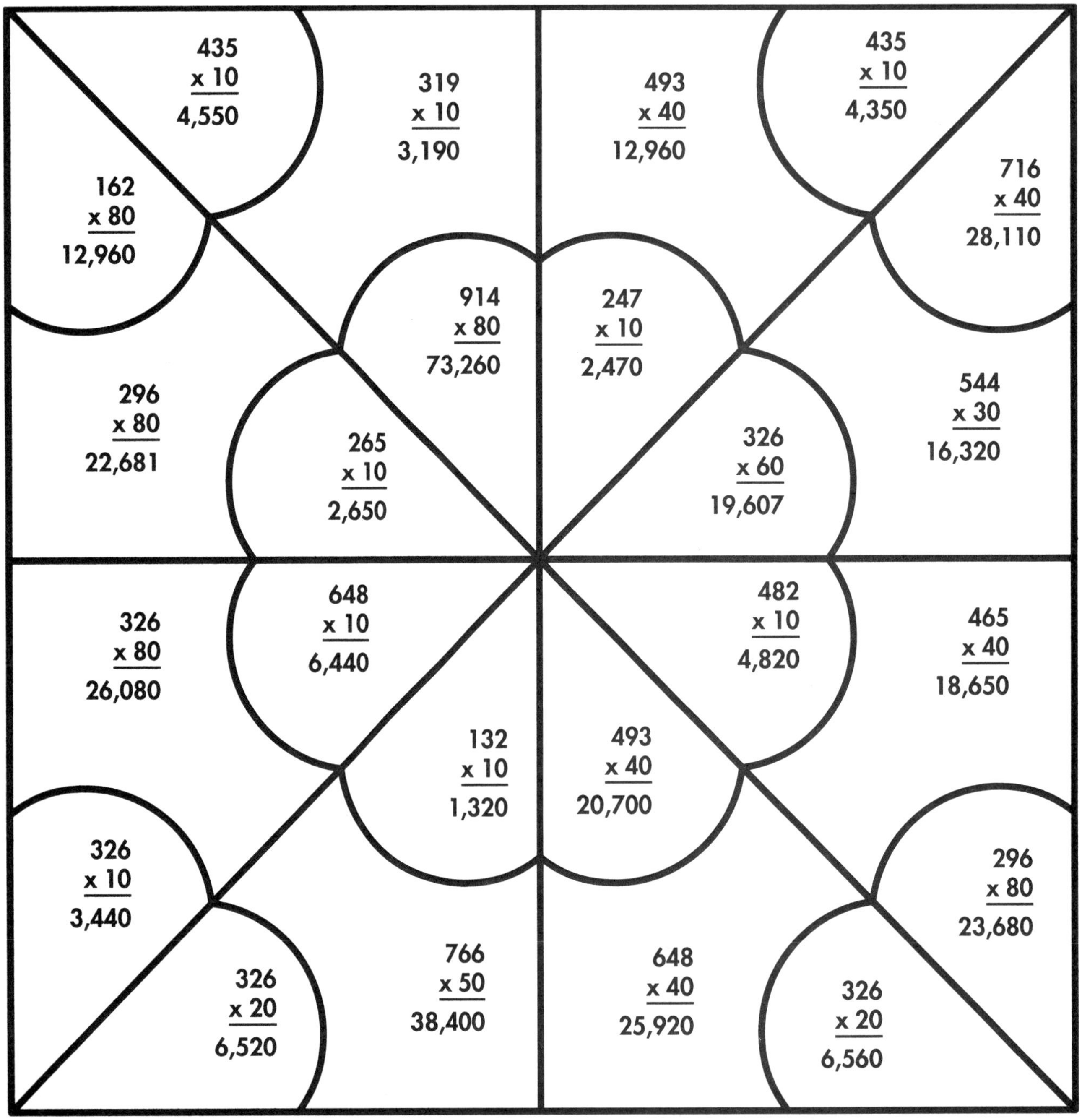

435
x 10
4,550

319
x 10
3,190

493
x 40
12,960

435
x 10
4,350

162
x 80
12,960

716
x 40
28,110

914
x 80
73,260

247
x 10
2,470

296
x 80
22,681

265
x 10
2,650

326
x 60
19,607

544
x 30
16,320

326
x 80
26,080

648
x 10
6,440

482
x 10
4,820

465
x 40
18,650

132
x 10
1,320

493
x 40
20,700

326
x 10
3,440

296
x 80
23,680

326
x 20
6,520

766
x 50
38,400

648
x 40
25,920

326
x 20
6,560

Color:

If the answer is correct, color the space red.

If the answer is wrong, color the space white.

This pattern may be named for board games that use spinners.

____

***C* Circle the numbers in the thousands place and box the numbers in the hundreds place.**

Rose Quilt

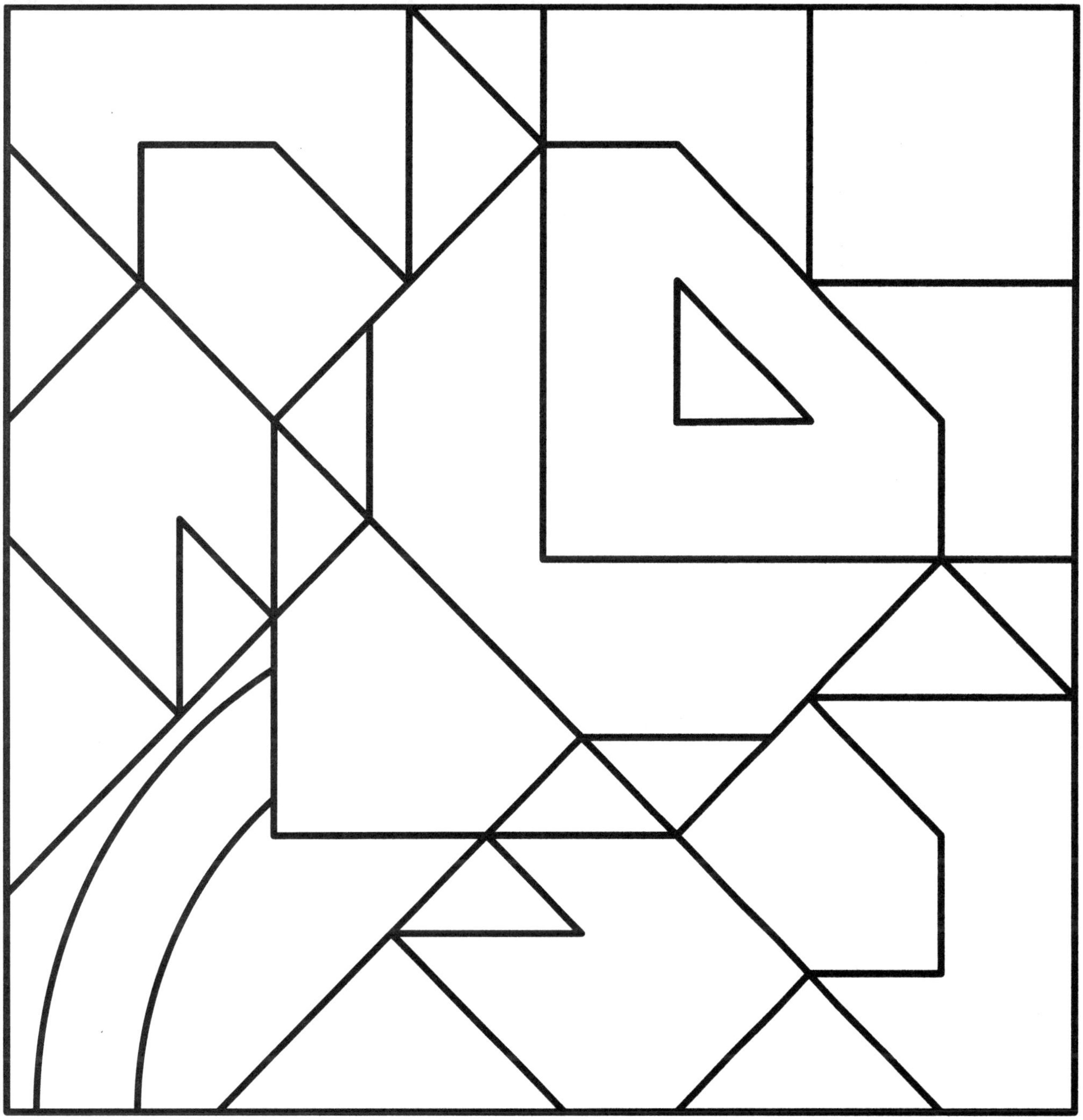

Use multiplication facts that your teacher gives you to create your own color code.

This is a modern quilt pattern. Can you find the rose?

Symbol

Quilt Name ______________________________

Use the shapes below to design a quilt pattern with a star shape. Then name the pattern and give a reason for the name you select.

Star of My Heart

$2\overline{)8}$ $2\overline{)14}$ $2\overline{)10}$ $2\overline{)18}$ $2\overline{)10}$

$2\overline{)16}$ $2\overline{)6}$ $1\overline{)8}$

$1\overline{)4}$ $2\overline{)12}$ $2\overline{)8}$

$2\overline{)18}$ $2\overline{)4}$ $1\overline{)7}$

$2\overline{)20}$ $2\overline{)18}$

$2\overline{)12}$ $1\overline{)5}$ $1\overline{)6}$

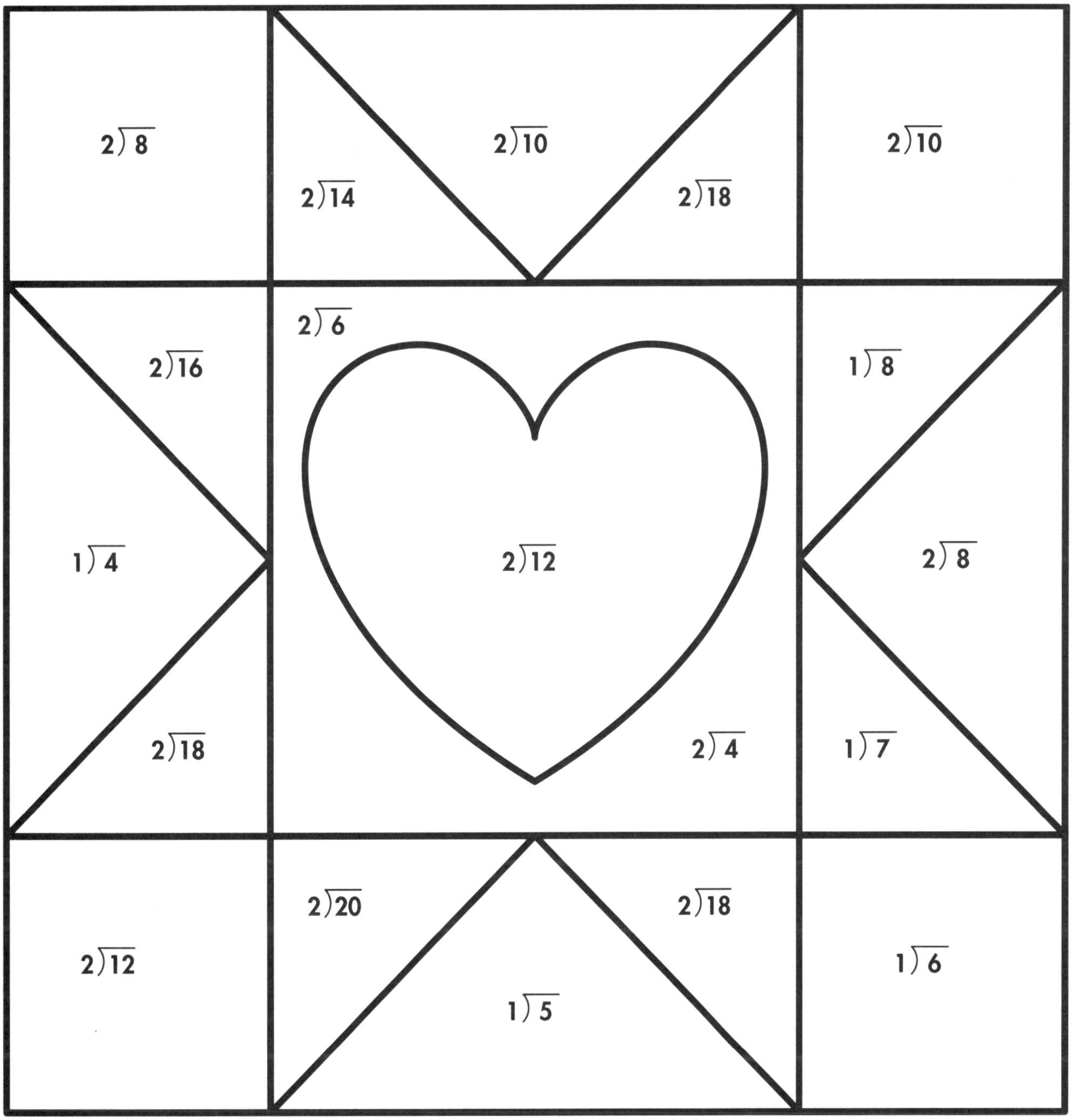

Color:

2 and 3 = yellow
4, 5, and 6 = red
7, 8, 9, and 10 = blue

In Colonial times, people sewed heart quilts for friends who were going to be married.

***C* If there are twelve cupcakes for two children, how many cupcakes will each child get?**

÷ 1, ÷ 2

Old Maid's Puzzle

8 ÷ 2

18 ÷ 2

7 ÷ 1

6 ÷ 1

8 ÷ 2

3 ÷ 1

20 ÷ 2

16 ÷ 2

10 ÷ 2

6 ÷ 2

12 ÷ 2

4 ÷ 2

10 ÷ 2

4 ÷ 2

18 ÷ 1

8 ÷ 1

1 ÷ 1

12 ÷ 2

8 ÷ 2

14 ÷ 2

20 ÷ 2

5 ÷ 1

Color:

1, 2, and 3 = brown
4, 5, and 6 = green
7 and 8 = yellow
9 and 10 = orange

A Colonial woman who wasn't married by the age of 25 was often considered an old maid.

***C* You have eighteen apples and want to put an equal number in two baskets. How many apples will you put in each basket?**

North Star

$3\overline{)3}$

$3\overline{)6}$

$3\overline{)9}$

$3\overline{)18}$

$3\overline{)12}$

$3\overline{)15}$

$3\overline{)21}$

$3\overline{)24}$

$3\overline{)18}$

$3\overline{)27}$

$3\overline{)30}$

$3\overline{)21}$

Color:

If the answer is even, color the space blue.

If the answer is odd, color the space white.

Many Pioneers could tell which direction they were going by locating the North Star in the sky.

***C* Write the division facts for three on the back of this sheet of paper.**

Delectable Mountains

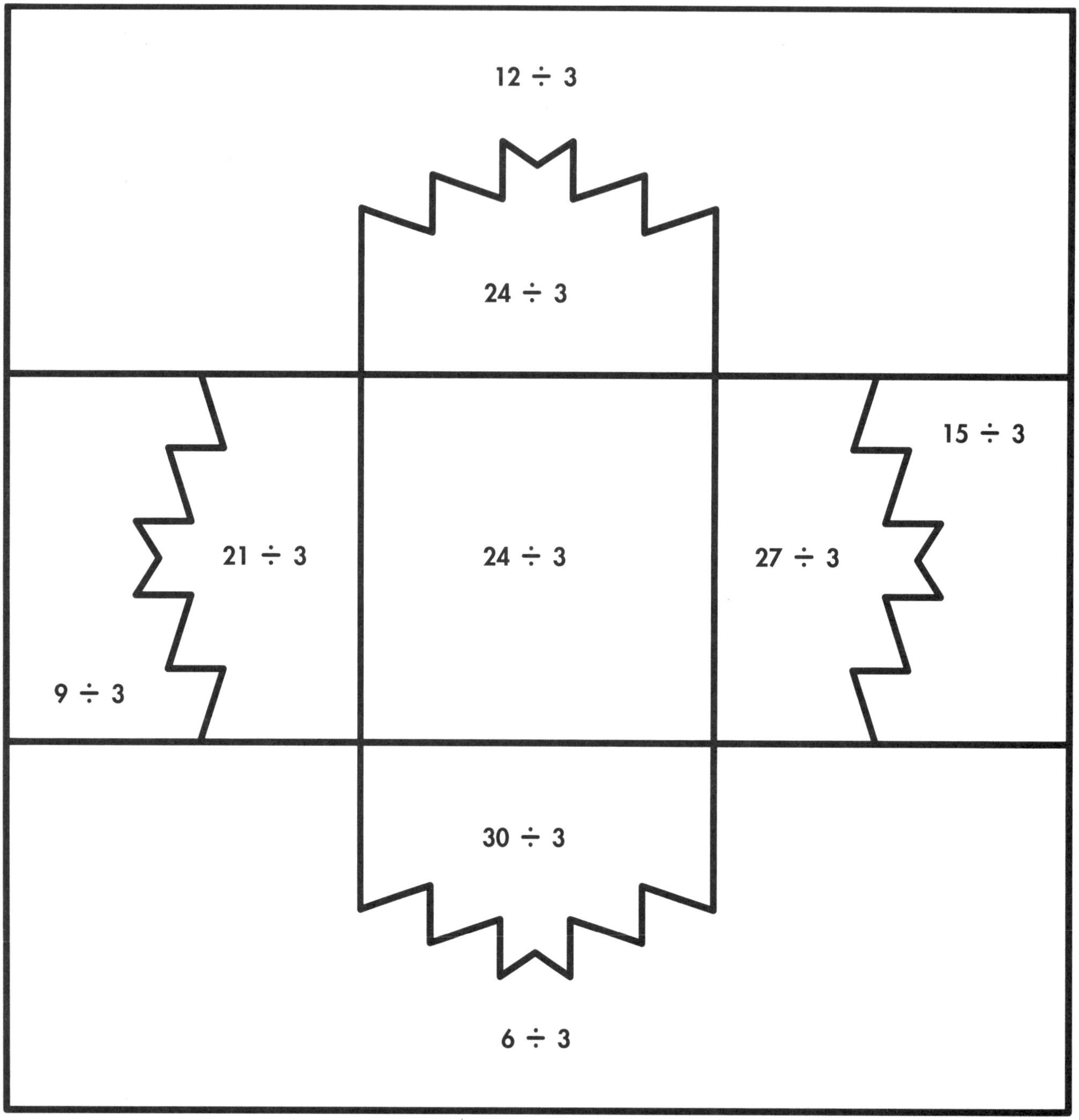

12 ÷ 3

24 ÷ 3

21 ÷ 3

24 ÷ 3

27 ÷ 3

15 ÷ 3

9 ÷ 3

30 ÷ 3

6 ÷ 3

Color:

If the answer is less than 6, color the space blue.

If the answer is more than 6, color the space green.

One of the books many pioneers read is called *Pilgrim's Progress*, by John Bunyan. Mountains are an important part of that book.

***C* Look on the map to locate a mountain range in the United States. Write its name on the back of this sheet of paper.**

Pennsylvania Dutch Design

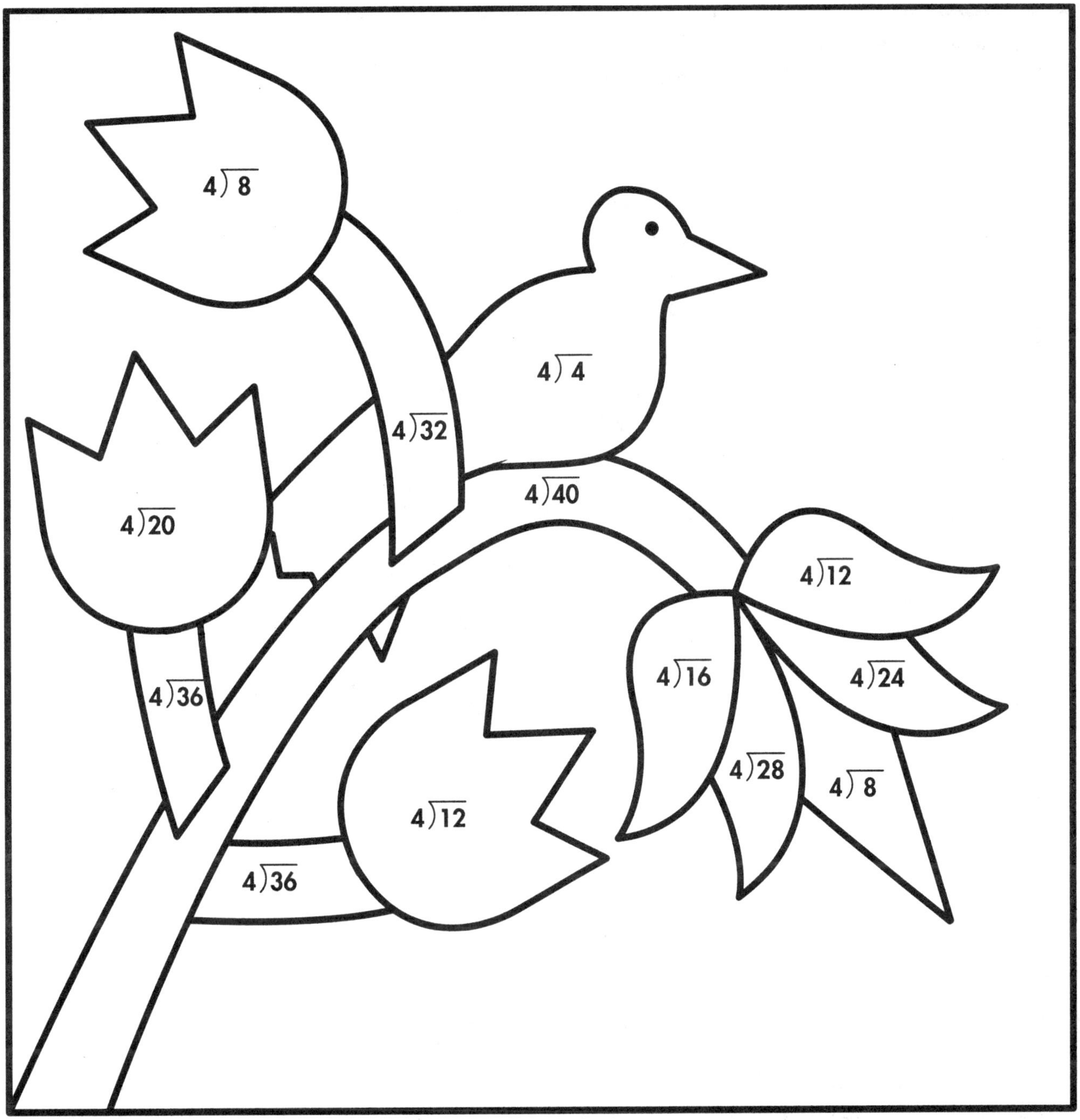

4)8

4)4

4)32

4)40

4)20

4)12

4)16

4)24

4)36

4)28

4)8

4)12

4)36

Color:

1 = blue
2, 3, and 4 = red
5, 6, and 7 = orange
8, 9, and 10 = green

Amish people use this pattern on dishes and signs as well as on quilts.

***C* Divide a dozen donuts by four. Write the answer on the back of this sheet of paper.**

Love of Arrowheads

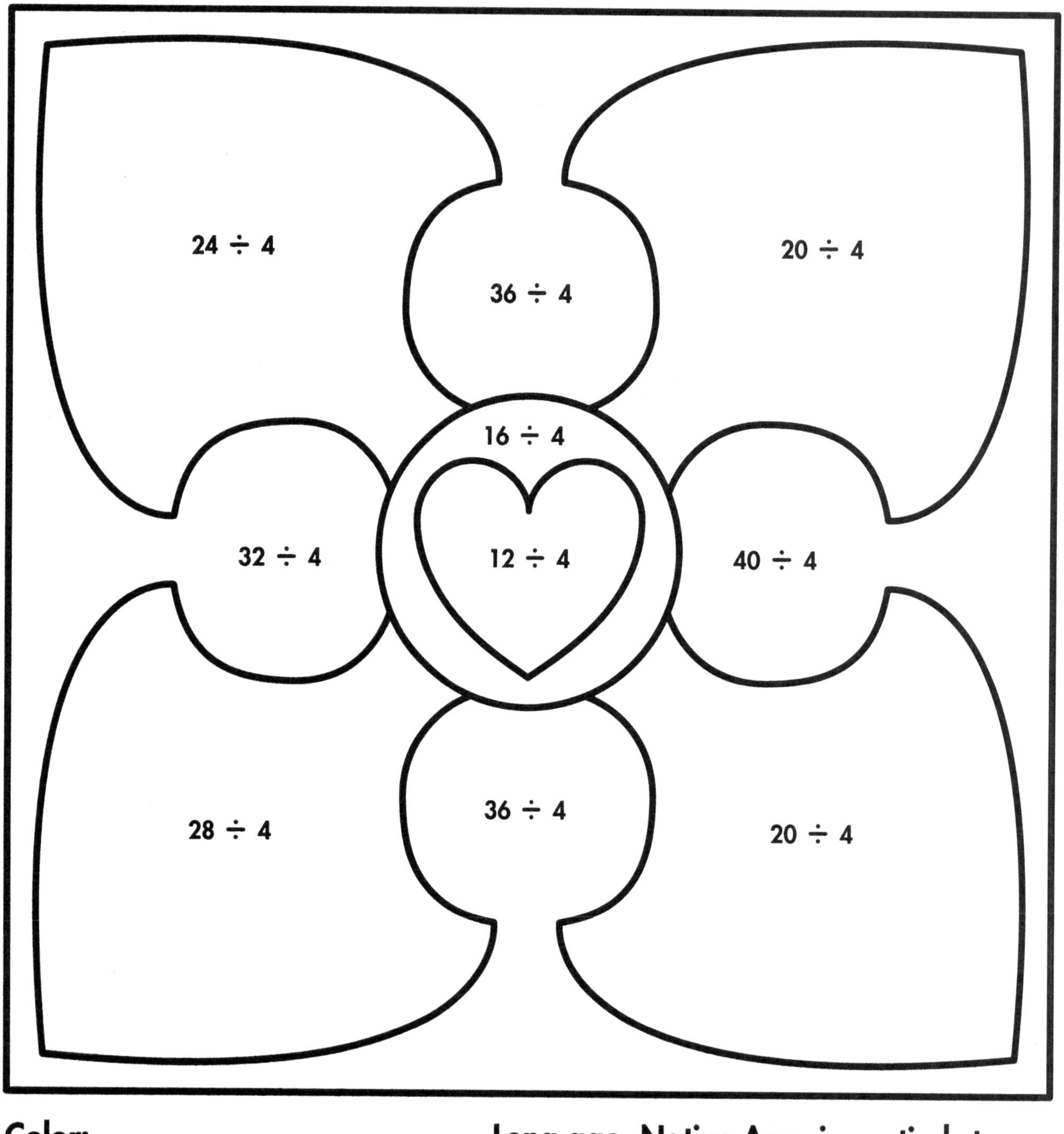

Color:

2 and 3 = red
4, 5, 6, and 7 = brown
8, 9, and 10 = yellow

Long ago, Native Americans tied stone tips to thin branches to make arrows. This is a modern quilt pattern.

***C* If you have twenty-four stones and want to make four even piles, how many stones will you put in each pile?**

Milady's Fan

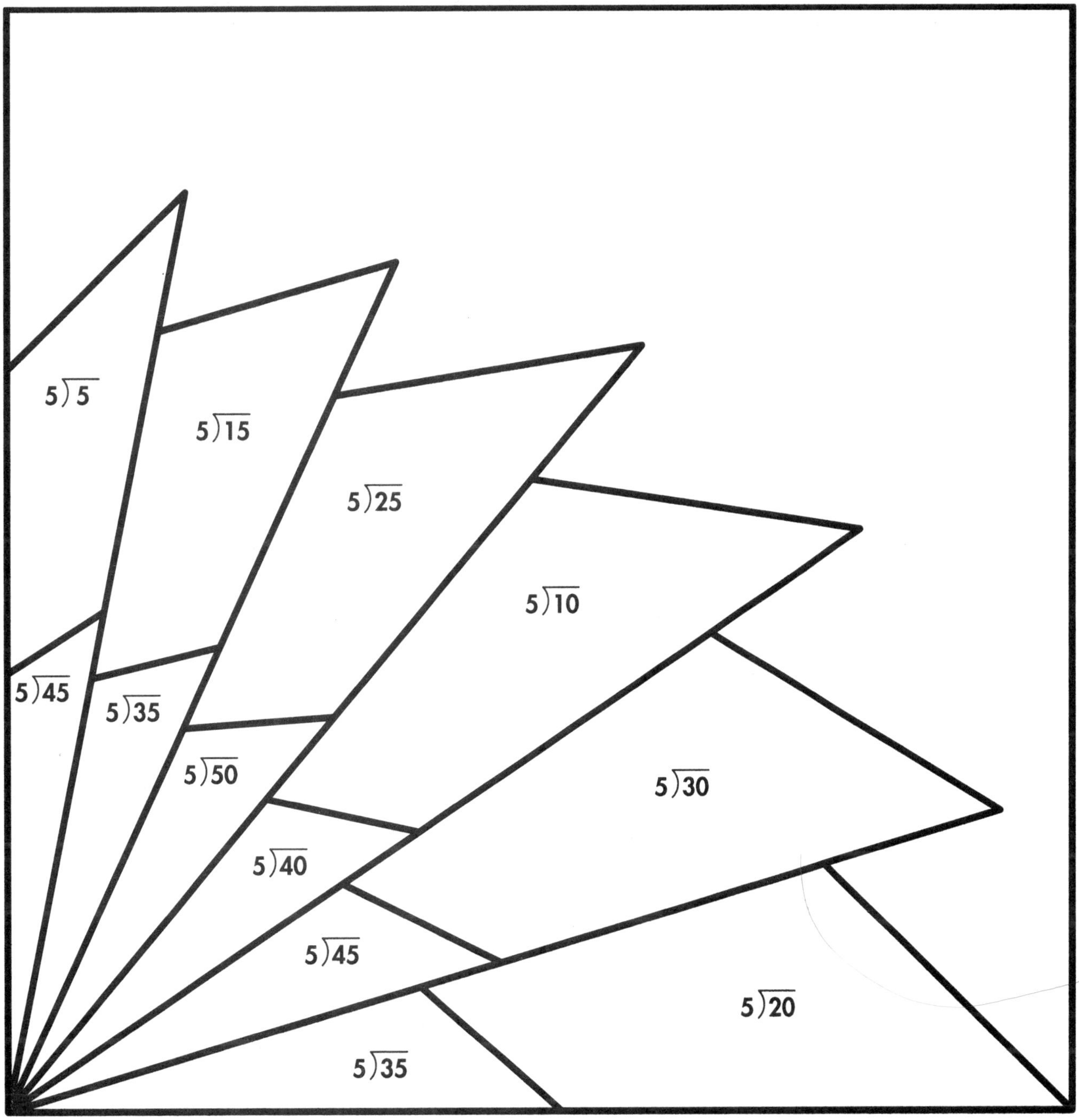

5)5

5)15

5)25

5)10

5)45

5)35

5)50

5)30

5)40

5)45

5)20

5)35

Color:

1 and 2 = red
3 and 4 = orange
5 and 6 = yellow
7 and 8 = green
9 and 10 = blue

In Colonial times, no lady was properly prepared for a social function unless she carried a fan.

***C* Count the children in your room. Divide that number by five. Write the answer on the back of this sheet of paper.**

Vee Block

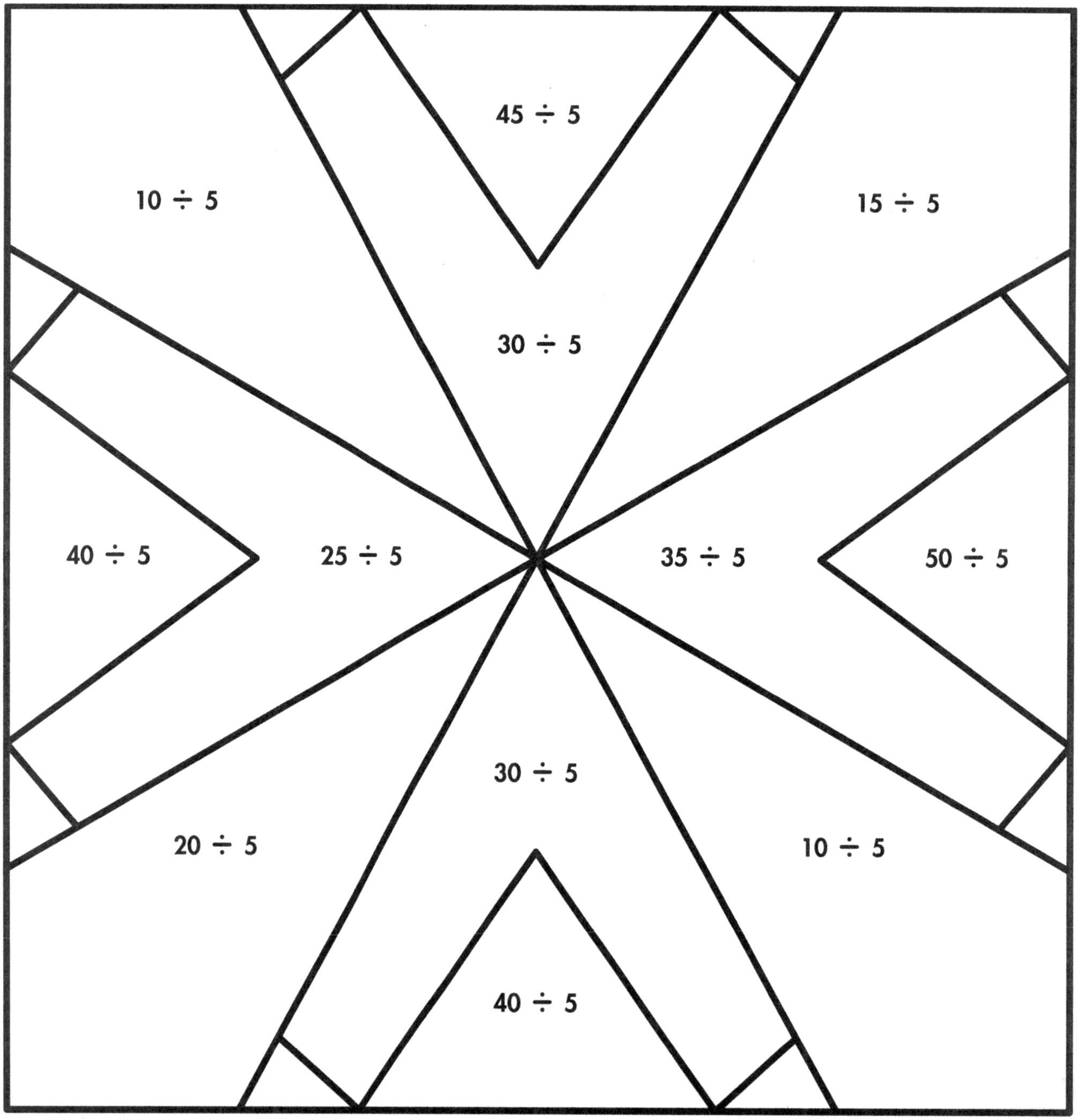

Color:

2, 3, and 4 = blue
5, 6, and 7 = blue
8, 9, and 10 = blue

This pattern is named for a letter in the alphabet.

____

***C* Skip-count by fives to one hundred fifty. Write the numbers on the back of this sheet of paper.**

Milky Way

÷ 1 to ÷ 5

4)24 4)28	4)4	5)35 5)40	2)8	3)18 2)20
5)10		2)6	5)5	5)25
4)32 2)18	3)9	5)40 5)45	4)8	4)28 3)18
5)20	4)20	3)3		3)6
4)40 5)30	3)12	5)40 3)21	4)12	3)27 3)30

Color:

If the answer is from 1 to 5, color the space yellow.

If the answer is from 6 to 10, color the space blue.

The Milky Way looks like a dim sprinkling of stars in the sky. It is made up of too many stars to count!

***C* Write the names of three planets on the back of this sheet of paper.**

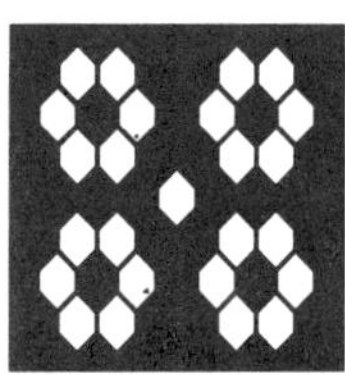

Grandmother's Flower Garden

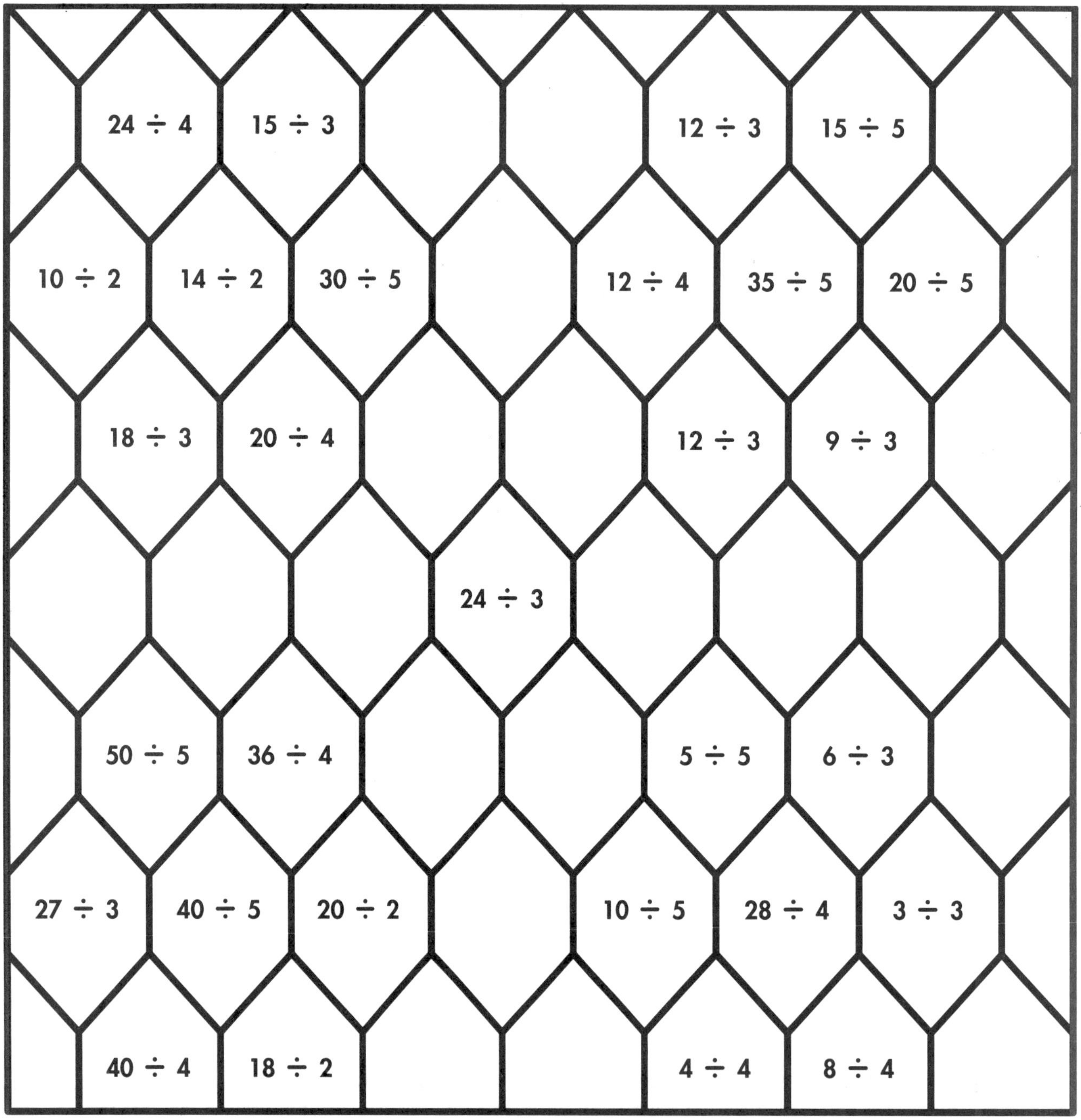

$24 \div 4$ $15 \div 3$ $12 \div 3$ $15 \div 5$

$10 \div 2$ $14 \div 2$ $30 \div 5$ $12 \div 4$ $35 \div 5$ $20 \div 5$

$18 \div 3$ $20 \div 4$ $12 \div 3$ $9 \div 3$

$24 \div 3$

$50 \div 5$ $36 \div 4$ $5 \div 5$ $6 \div 3$

$27 \div 3$ $40 \div 5$ $20 \div 2$ $10 \div 5$ $28 \div 4$ $3 \div 3$

$40 \div 4$ $18 \div 2$ $4 \div 4$ $8 \div 4$

Color:

1 and 2 = green
3 and 4 = orange
5 and 6 = red
7 and 8 = yellow
9 and 10 = blue

This pattern was designed to show the brightly colored flowers in Grandma's garden. Another name for this pattern is Beehive.

***C* On the back of this sheet of paper, write about a flower garden you have seen.**

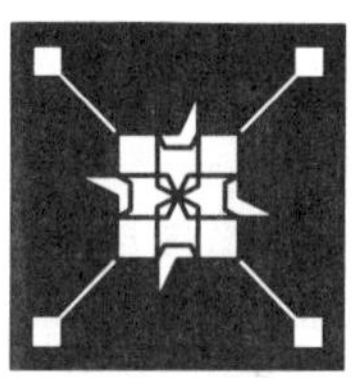

The Farmer's Wife

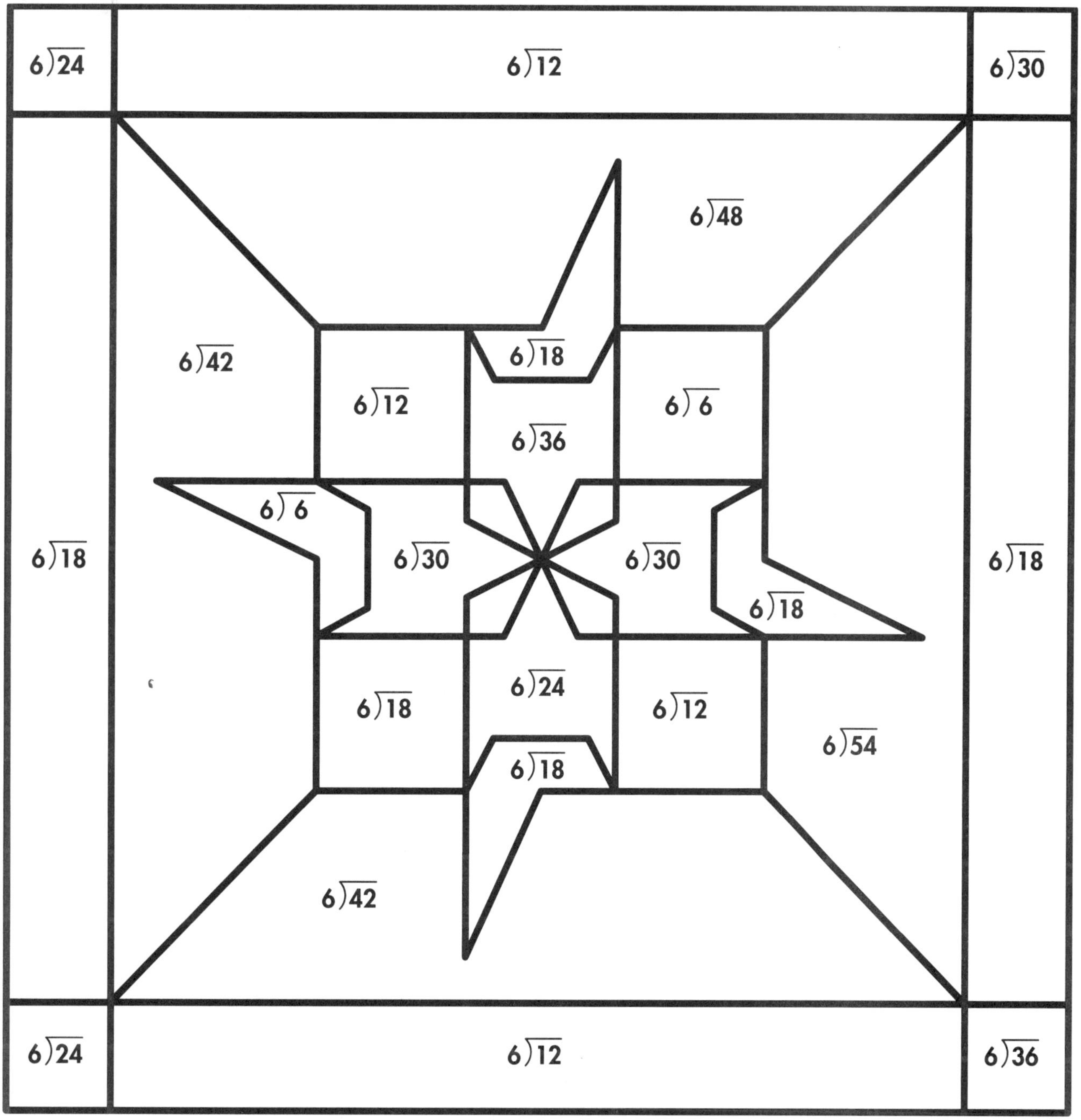

6)24
6)12
6)30
6)48
6)42
6)18
6)12
6)6
6)36
6)6
6)18
6)30
6)30
6)18
6)18
6)24
6)18
6)12
6)54
6)18
6)42
6)24
6)12
6)36

Color:

1, 2, and 3 = purple
4, 5, and 6 = yellow
7, 8, and 9 = green

A farmer's wife, stitching a quilt through the long, cold winter, may have named this picture for herself.

***C* Write the division facts for six on the back of this sheet of paper.**

Rocky Road to Dublin

6 ÷ 6 12 ÷ 6	18 ÷ 6 24 ÷ 6	24 ÷ 6 18 ÷ 6	30 ÷ 6 12 ÷ 6
36 ÷ 6 54 ÷ 6	12 ÷ 6 42 ÷ 6	60 ÷ 6 30 ÷ 6	54 ÷ 6 48 ÷ 6
60 ÷ 6 54 ÷ 6	42 ÷ 6 48 ÷ 6	30 ÷ 6 36 ÷ 6	18 ÷ 6 12 ÷ 6
36 ÷ 6 30 ÷ 6	42 ÷ 6 48 ÷ 6	60 ÷ 6 54 ÷ 6	24 ÷ 6 18 ÷ 6

Color:

If the answer is even,
color the space purple.
If the answer is odd,
color the space green.

After 1849, this pattern was renamed the Rocky Road to California. That was the year many people rushed to California to look for gold.

***C* How many six-cent whistles can you buy with twenty-four cents?**

Missouri Star

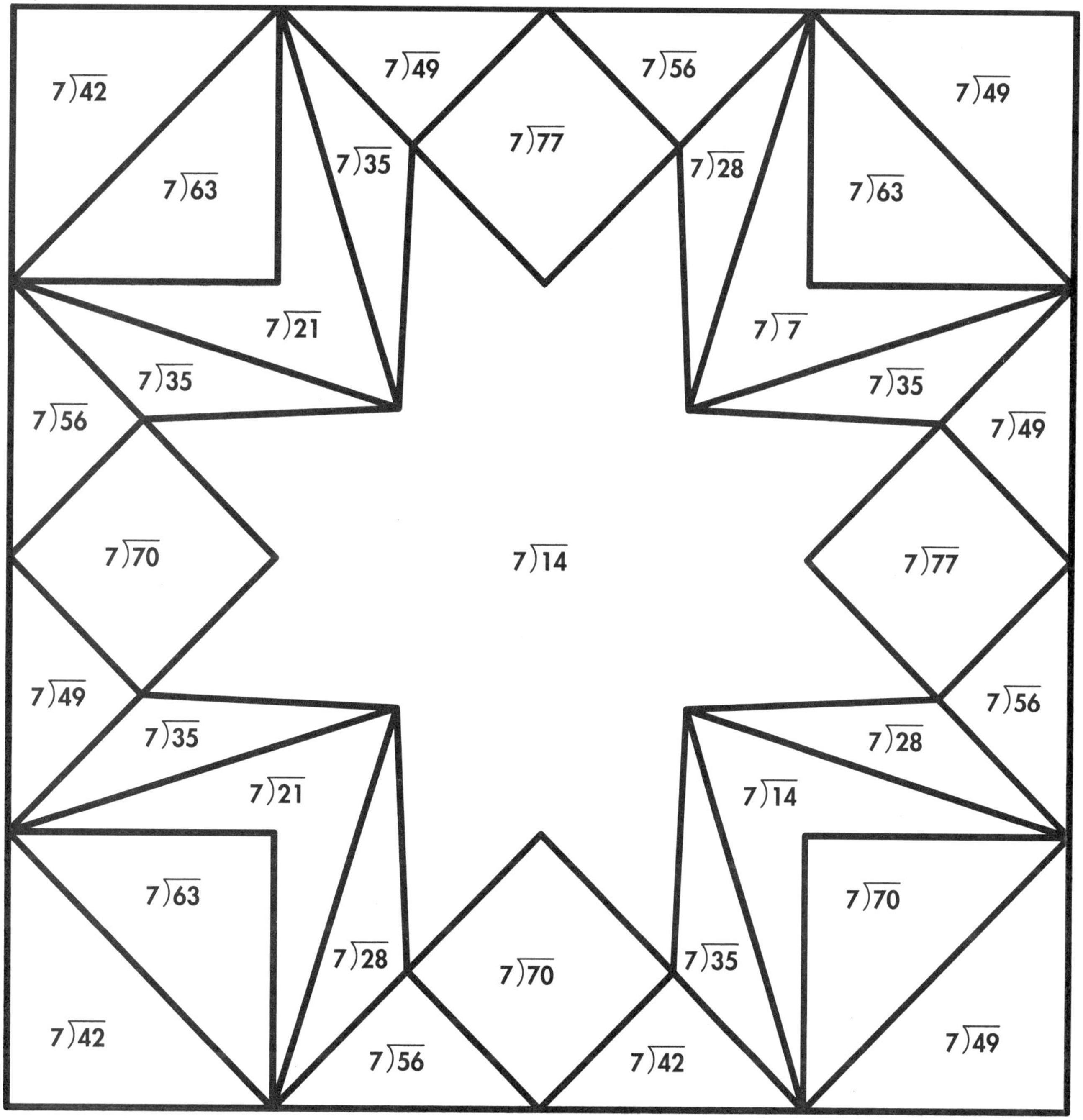

7)49 7)56

7)42 7)49

7)77

7)35 7)28

7)63 7)63

7)21 7)7

7)35 7)35

7)56 7)49

7)70 7)14 7)77

7)49 7)56

7)35 7)28

7)21 7)14

7)63 7)70

7)28 7)70 7)35

7)42 7)49

7)56 7)42

Color:

1, 2, and 3 = yellow
4 and 5 = green
6, 7, and 8 = black
9 and 10 = red

This design was named to honor the state of Missouri.

***C* On the back of this sheet of paper, write the name of the capital of Missouri.**

Dobbins Fan

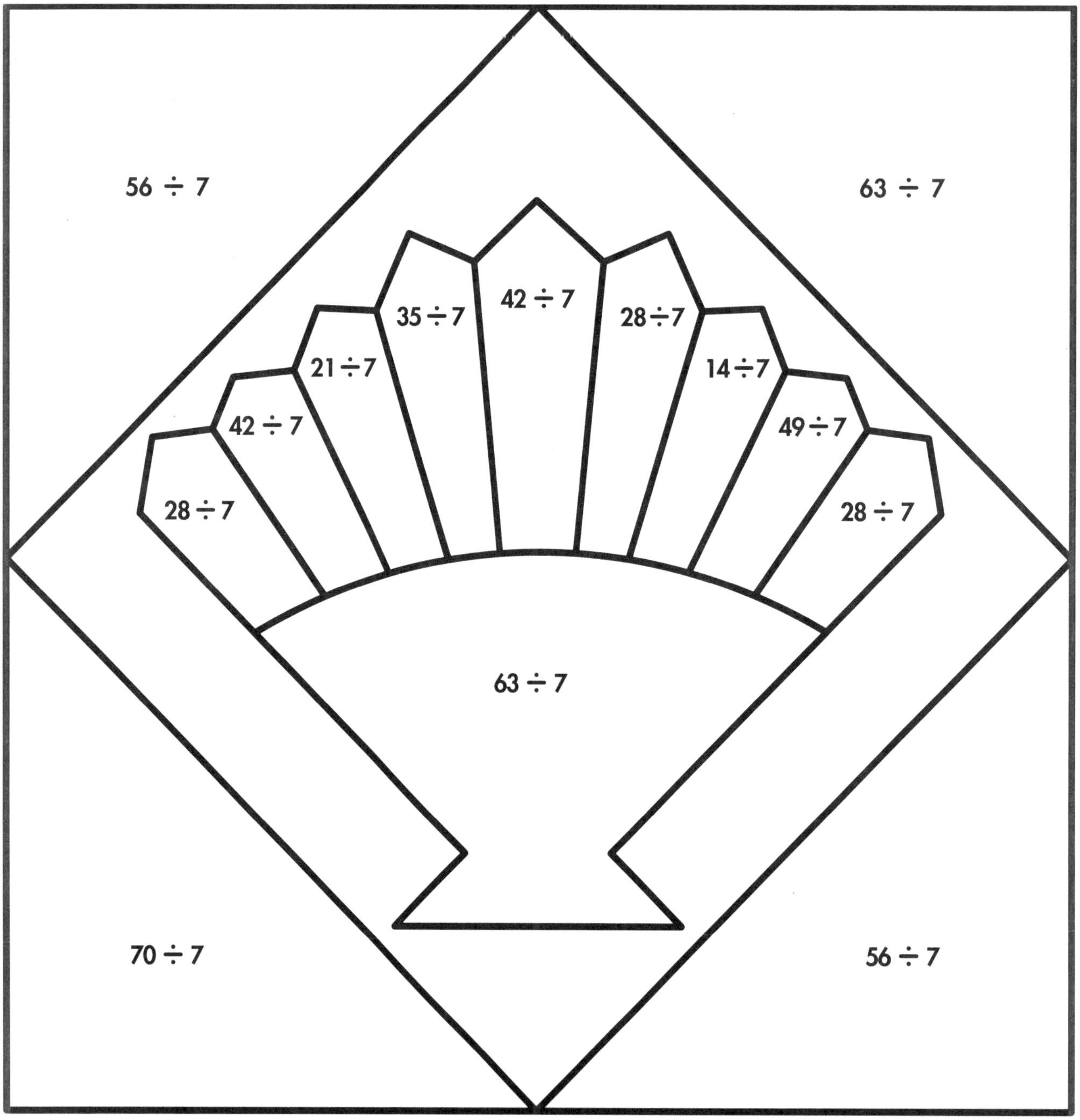

56 ÷ 7

63 ÷ 7

42 ÷ 7

35 ÷ 7

28 ÷ 7

21 ÷ 7

14 ÷ 7

42 ÷ 7

49 ÷ 7

28 ÷ 7

28 ÷ 7

63 ÷ 7

70 ÷ 7

56 ÷ 7

Color:

2 and 3 = yellow
4 and 5 = blue
6 and 7 = green
8, 9, and 10 = red

Quite often a design is named for the person who puts it in a quilt. Someone with the last name Dobbins may have been the first in her town to use this pattern.

***C* Write the division facts for seven on the back of this sheet of paper.**

Queen's Pride

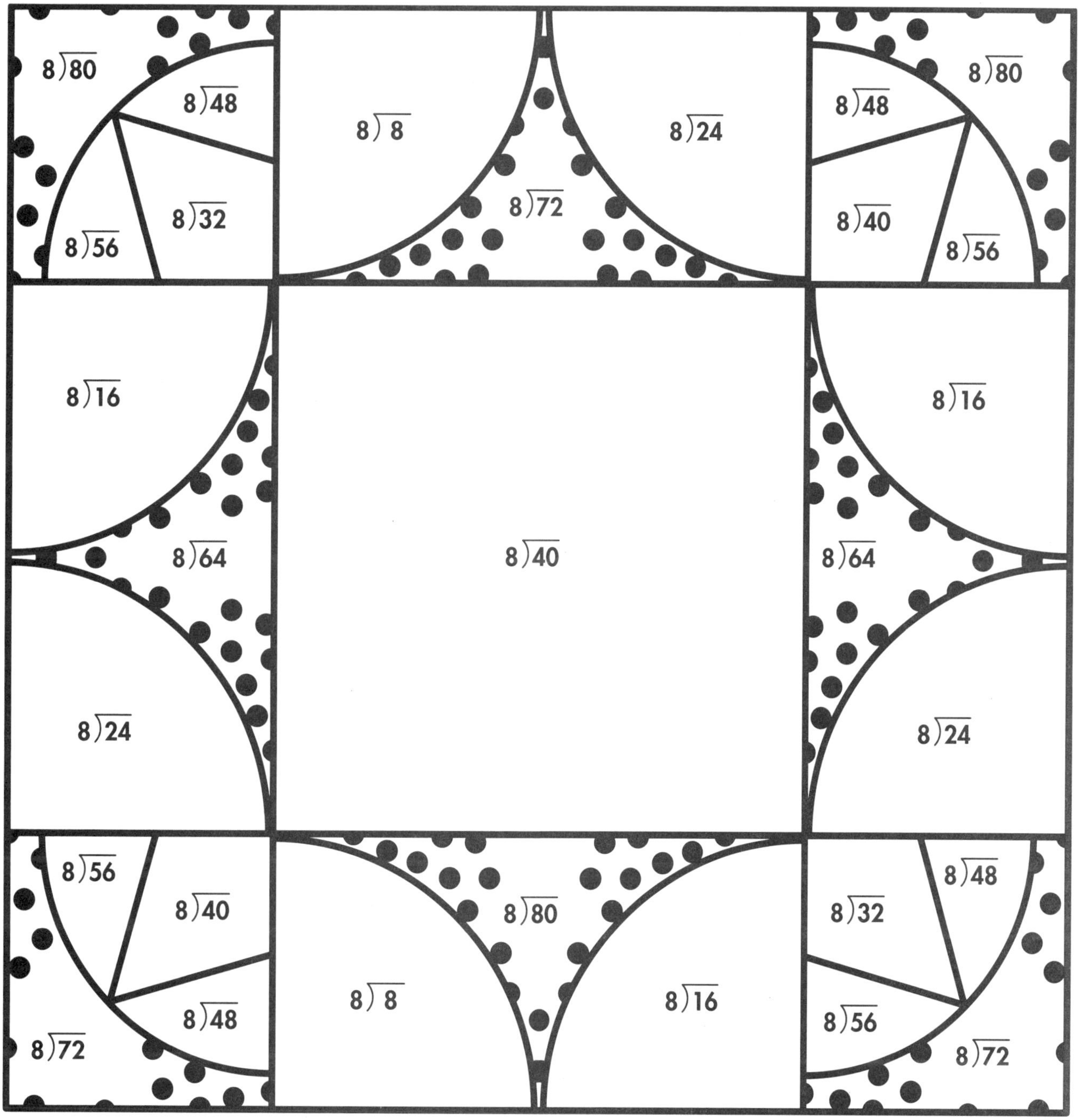

8)80 8)48 8)32 8)56

8)8 8)24 8)72

8)80 8)48 8)40 8)56

8)16 8)64 8)24

8)40

8)16 8)64 8)24

8)56 8)40 8)48 8)72

8)80 8)8 8)16

8)48 8)32 8)56 8)72

Color:

1, 2, and 3 = green
4 and 5 = blue
6 and 7 = yellow
8, 9, and 10 = orange

This quilt design may have been named to honor a queen.

***C* On the back of this sheet of paper, write the multiplication and division facts for eight.**

Golden Gate

72 ÷ 8	8 ÷ 8		32 ÷ 8 64 ÷ 8 48 ÷ 8	24 ÷ 8	80 ÷ 8		
40 ÷ 8	56 ÷ 8	48 ÷ 8	16 ÷ 8	40 ÷ 8	56 ÷ 8	48 ÷ 8	
16 ÷ 8	80 ÷ 8		32 ÷ 8 64 ÷ 8 40 ÷ 8	24 ÷ 8	72 ÷ 8		

Color:
- 1, 2, and 3 = brown
- 4, 5, and 6 = green
- 7 and 8 = yellow
- 9 and 10 = blue

This design was a great favorite of many pioneer brides-to-be.

***C* On the back of this sheet of paper, write the name of the state where the Golden Gate Bridge is located.**

Bridal Stairway

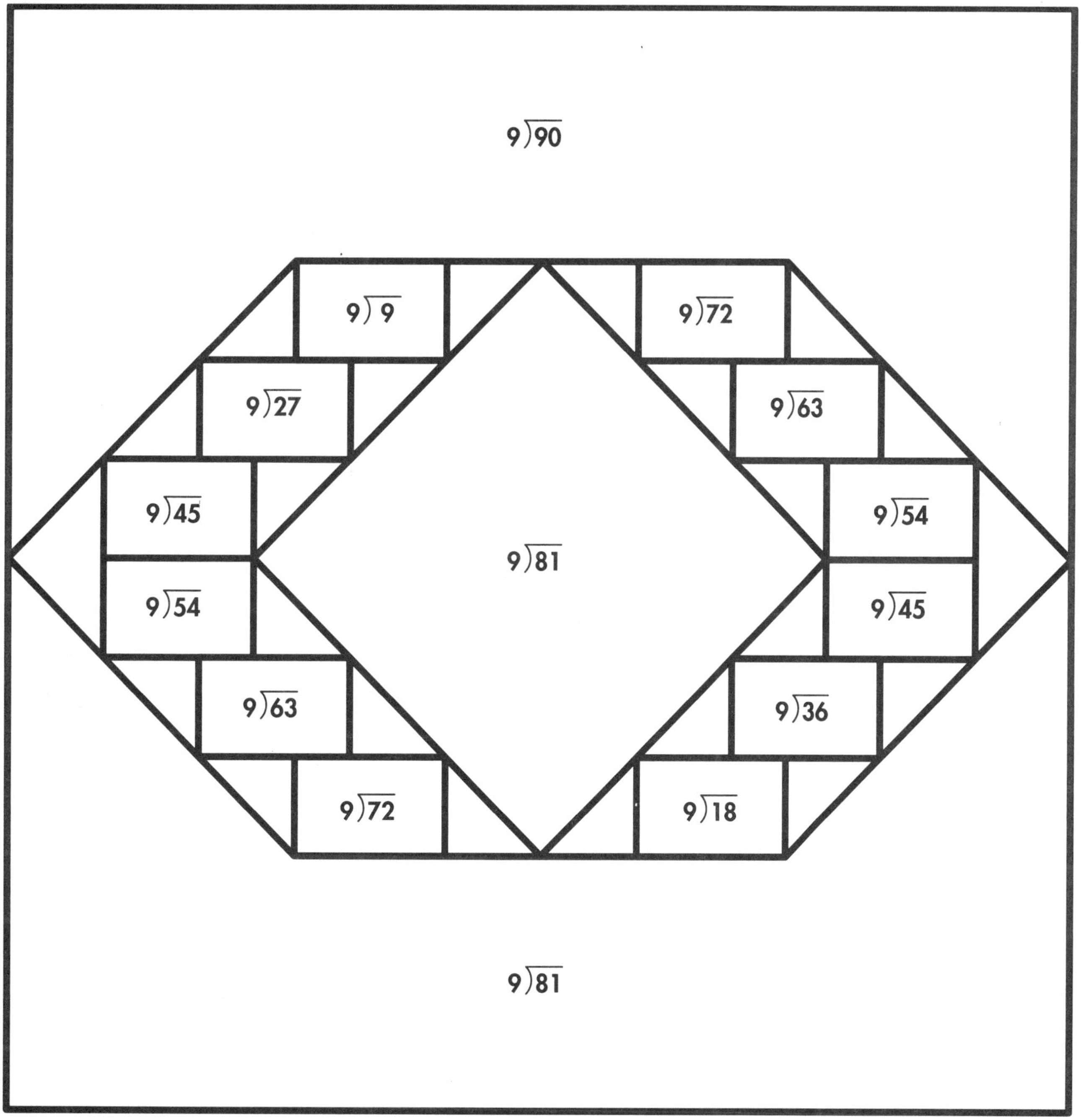

$9\overline{)90}$

$9\overline{)9}$ $9\overline{)72}$

$9\overline{)27}$ $9\overline{)63}$

$9\overline{)45}$ $9\overline{)54}$

$9\overline{)81}$

$9\overline{)54}$ $9\overline{)45}$

$9\overline{)63}$ $9\overline{)36}$

$9\overline{)72}$ $9\overline{)18}$

$9\overline{)81}$

Color:
1 and 2 = red
3 and 4 = orange
5 = yellow
6 = green
7 = blue
8 = purple
9 and 10 = brown

This pattern is named for the walk brides take down a church aisle.

***C* If you have thirty-six hot dogs to give to nine children, how many will each child get?**

Sawtooth

Color:

If the answer is odd, color the space white.
If the answer is even, color the space green.

This pattern dates from the early 1800s. It is named for a carpenter's saw.

***C* Write the division facts for nine on the back of this sheet of paper.**

Vine of Friendship

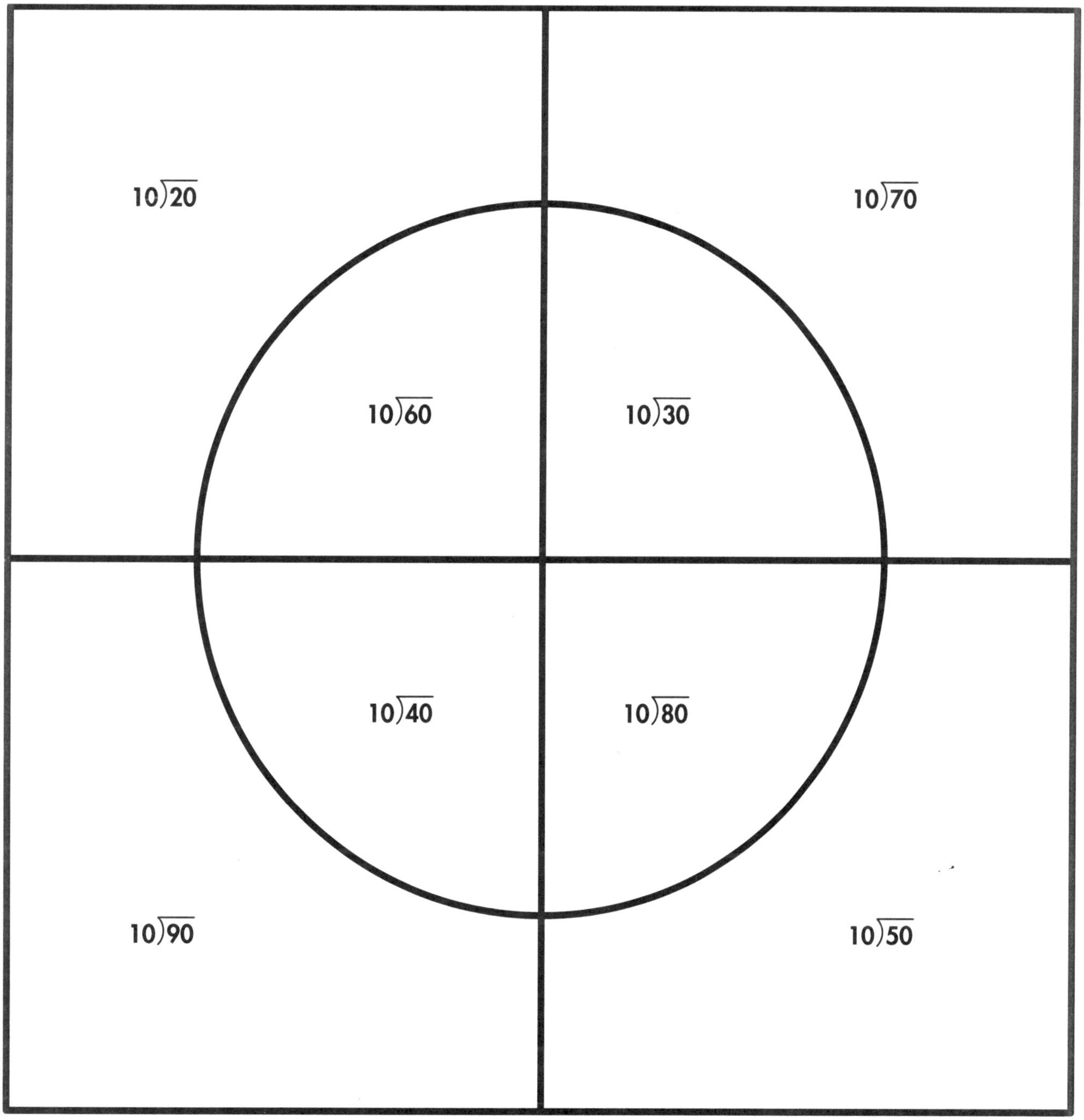

$10\overline{)20}$	$10\overline{)70}$
$10\overline{)60}$	$10\overline{)30}$
$10\overline{)40}$	$10\overline{)80}$
$10\overline{)90}$	$10\overline{)50}$

Color:

If the answer is from 1 to 5, color the space blue.

If the answer is from 6 to 9, color the space purple.

This pattern honors a close relationship between friends.

C Write the division facts for ten on the back of this sheet of paper.

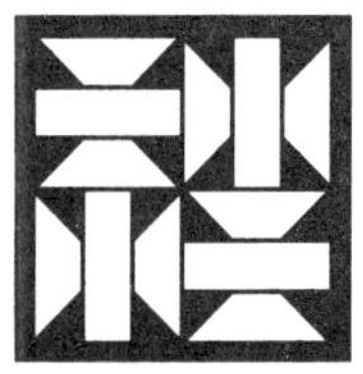

Arkansas Traveler

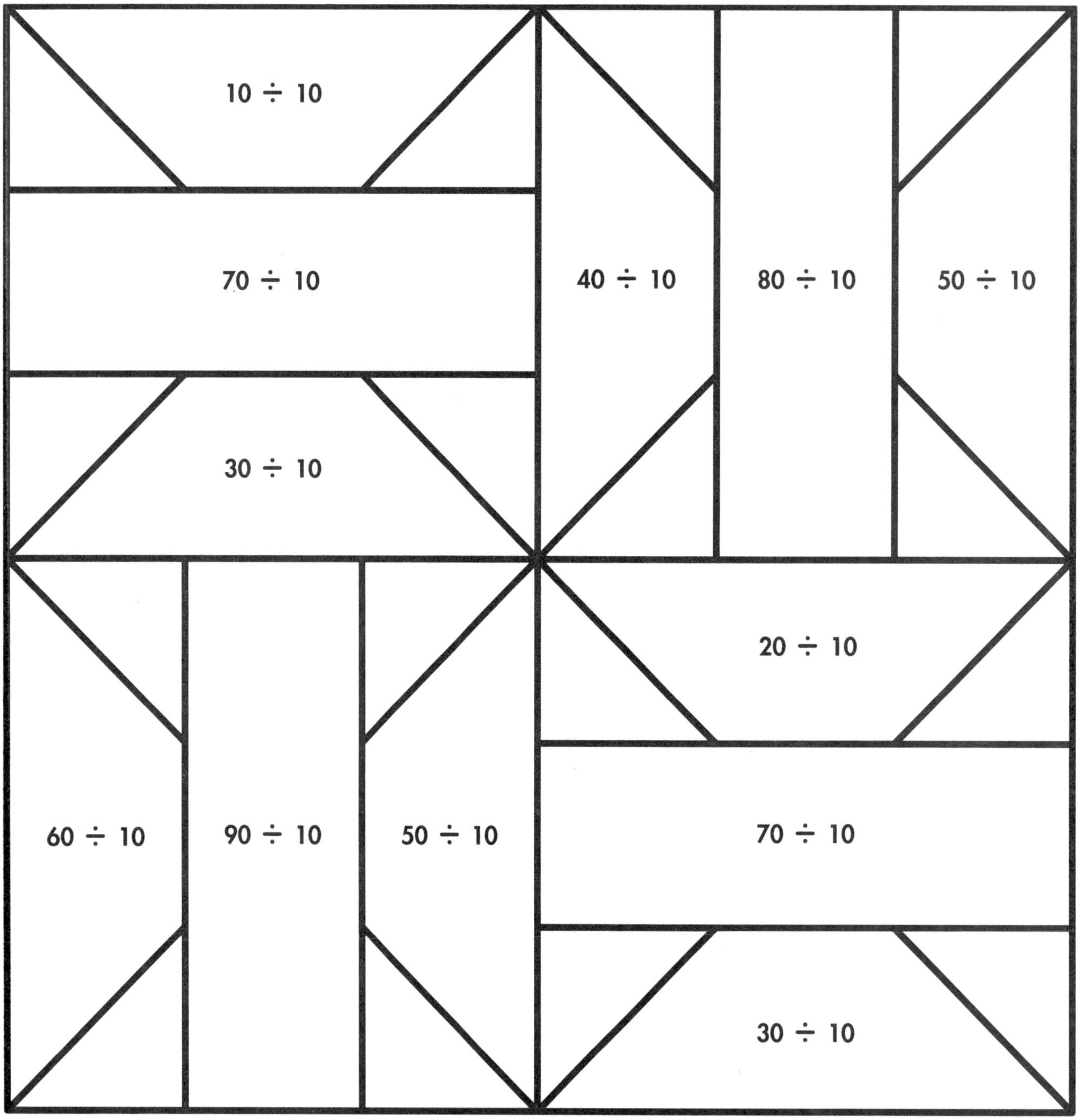

Color:

1, 2, and 3 = red
4, 5, and 6 = purple
7, 8, and 9 = green

Named to honor the state of Arkansas, this pattern is also called the Travel Star.

***C* Write the name of the capital of Arkansas on the back of this sheet of paper.**

Desert Bloom

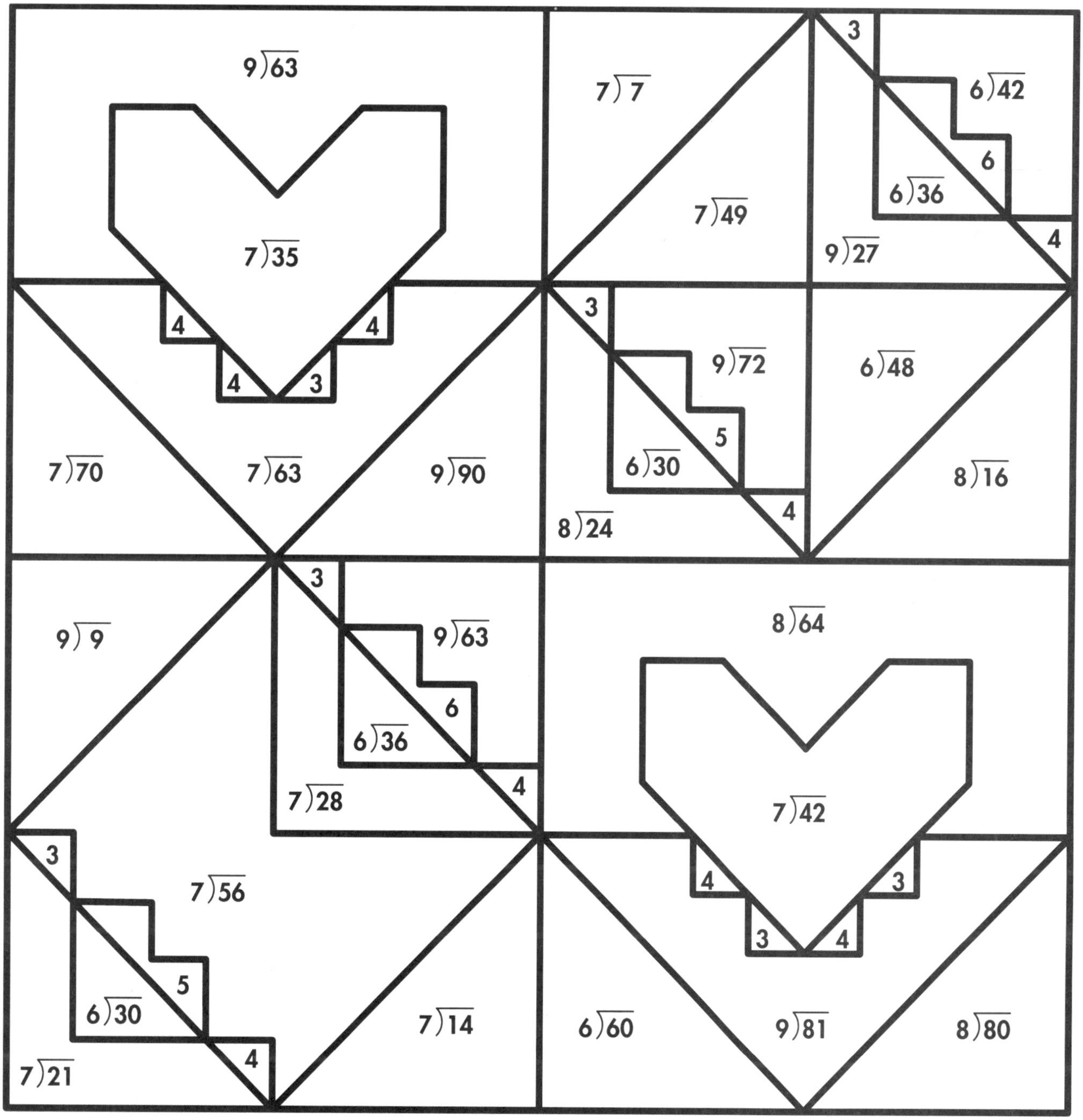

9)63 7)7 3 6)42
6 6)36
7)49
7)35 9)27 4

3
4 4 9)72 6)48
4 3
5
7)70 7)63 9)90 6)30 8)16
4
8)24

3
9)9 9)63 8)64
6
6)36
4
7)28 7)42

3 4 3
7)56
3 4
5
6)30 7)14 6)60 9)81 8)80
4
7)21

Color:

1 and 2 = orange
3 and 4 = yellow
5 and 6 = purple
7 and 8 = brown
9 = green
10 = red

The plants and colors of the American Southwest inspired this design.

C Name two states that have a desert. Write them on the back of this sheet of paper.

Mexican Cross

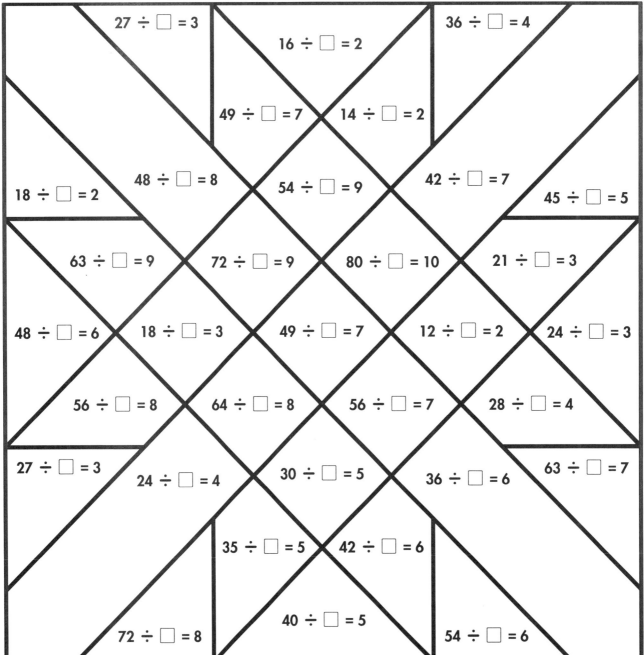

27 ÷ □ = 3
16 ÷ □ = 2
36 ÷ □ = 4
49 ÷ □ = 7
14 ÷ □ = 2
48 ÷ □ = 8
54 ÷ □ = 9
42 ÷ □ = 7
18 ÷ □ = 2
45 ÷ □ = 5
63 ÷ □ = 9
72 ÷ □ = 9
80 ÷ □ = 10
21 ÷ □ = 3
48 ÷ □ = 6
18 ÷ □ = 3
49 ÷ □ = 7
12 ÷ □ = 2
24 ÷ □ = 3
56 ÷ □ = 8
64 ÷ □ = 8
56 ÷ □ = 7
28 ÷ □ = 4
27 ÷ □ = 3
24 ÷ □ = 4
30 ÷ □ = 5
36 ÷ □ = 6
63 ÷ □ = 7
35 ÷ □ = 5
42 ÷ □ = 6
40 ÷ □ = 5
72 ÷ □ = 8
54 ÷ □ = 6

Color:

Put in the missing number to complete the problems.

6 = red
7 = yellow
8 = blue
9 = green

Can you see why this design is also called the Star and the Cross?

____

***C* Write the colors of the Mexican flag on the back of this sheet of paper.**

Clamshell

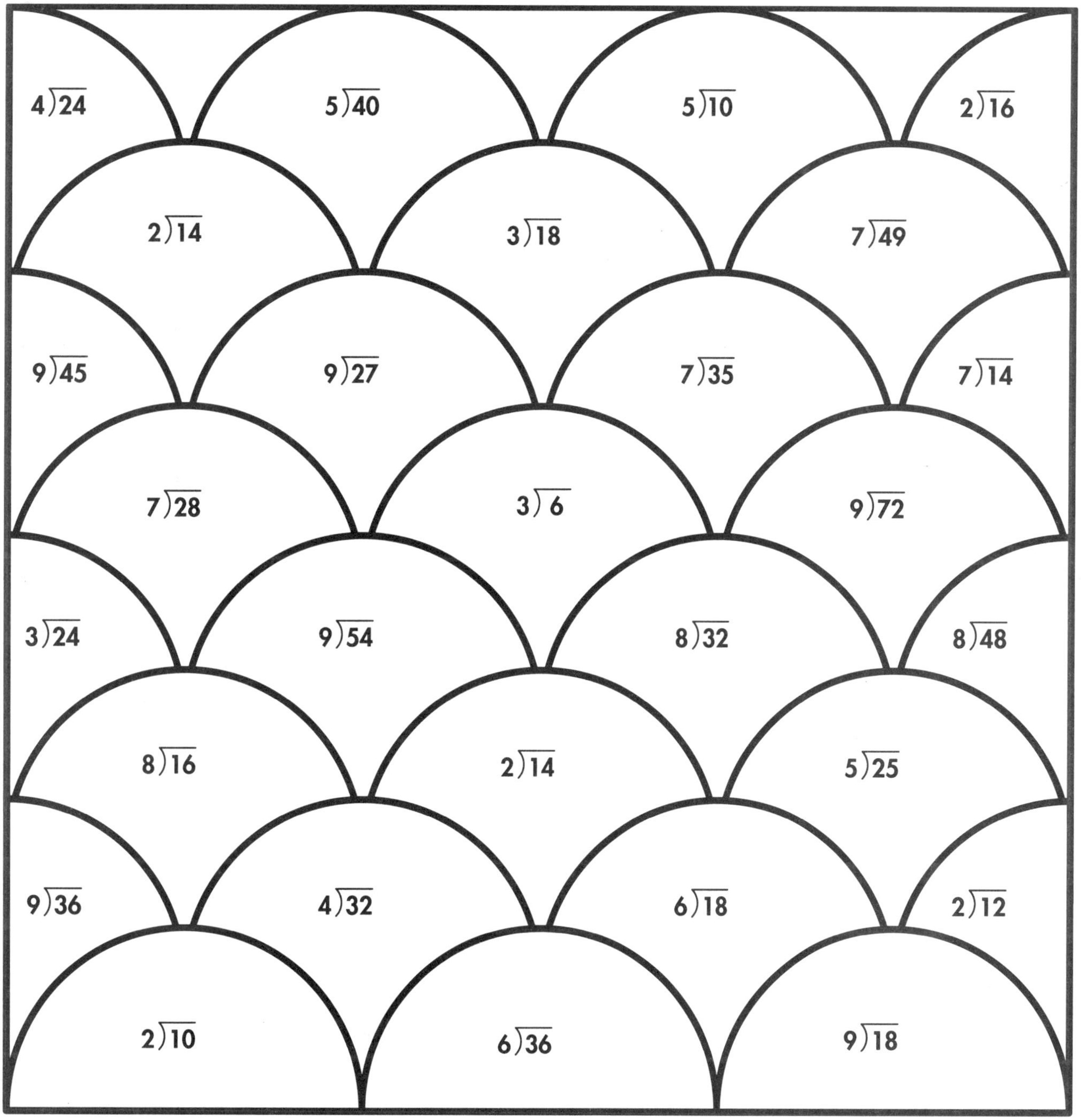

4)24 5)40 5)10 2)16

2)14 3)18 7)49

9)45 9)27 7)35 7)14

7)28 3)6 9)72

3)24 9)54 8)32 8)48

8)16 2)14 5)25

9)36 4)32 6)18 2)12

2)10 6)36 9)18

Color:
- 2 = red
- 3 = orange
- 4 = blue
- 5 = yellow
- 6 = green
- 7 = purple
- 8 = black

This Colonial design was popular among quiltmakers who lived near the Potomac River. Many people dug for clams along the riverbank.

***C* Find the Potomac River on the map. On the back of this sheet of paper, write the name of a famous city it runs by.**

Battle of the Alamo

21 ÷ 3 = 7
42 ÷ 6 = 6
6 ÷ 3 = 2
36 ÷ 3 = 3
63 ÷ 7 = 9

46 ÷ 6 = 8
20 ÷ 5 = 5
14 ÷ 2 = 8
21 ÷ 3 = 8
72 ÷ 9 = 8
40 ÷ 8 = 6

54 ÷ 6 = 9
49 ÷ 7 = 7
18 ÷ 9 = 3
49 ÷ 7 = 8
10 ÷ 2 = 4
81 ÷ 9 = 9
6 ÷ 3 = 1
8 ÷ 4 = 2

24 ÷ 4 = 6
72 ÷ 8 = 6
90 ÷ 9 = 10
80 ÷ 8 = 11
63 ÷ 9 = 8
27 ÷ 3 = 8
27 ÷ 9 = 3
36 ÷ 4 = 9

42 ÷ 7 = 5
30 ÷ 5 = 6
30 ÷ 5 = 8
15 ÷ 3 = 6
16 ÷ 4 = 3
42 ÷ 7 = 6
12 ÷ 6 = 2

30 ÷ 6 = 5
36 ÷ 6 = 7
36 ÷ 6 = 6
9 ÷ 3 = 4

Color:

If the answer is correct, color the space blue.
If the answer is wrong, color the space white.

This pattern honors a battle that was fought at the Alamo in Texas.

***C* On the back of this sheet of paper, write ten division facts that you are having trouble remembering.**

Divide 2 digits by 1 digit. No remainder.

Strawberry Patch

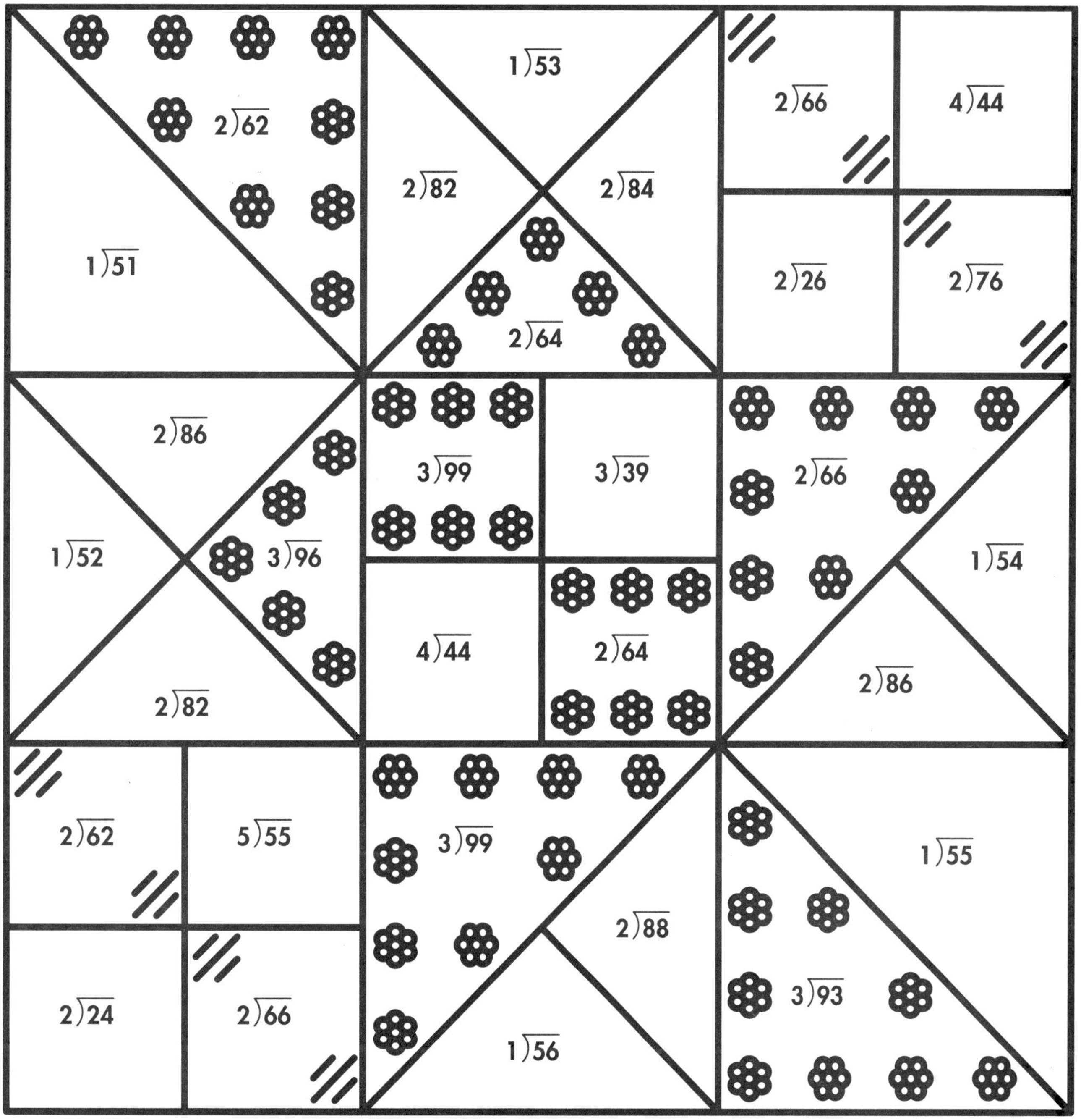

1)53 2)66 4)44 2)62 2)82 2)84 1)51 2)26 2)76 2)64

2)86 3)99 3)39 2)66 1)52 3)96 1)54 4)44 2)64 2)86 2)82

2)62 5)55 3)99 1)55 2)88 2)24 2)66 3)93 1)56

Color:

If the answer is from 11 to 20, color the space green.

If the answer is from 31 to 40, color the space pink.

If the answer is from 41 to 50, color the space orange.

If the answer is from 51 to 60, color the space red.

Many people grow strawberries in their gardens and make jam and syrup from the berries.

C Select one problem to write in number words instead of numerals. Write it on the back of this sheet of paper.

Divide 2 digits by 1 digit. No remainder.

Sunburst

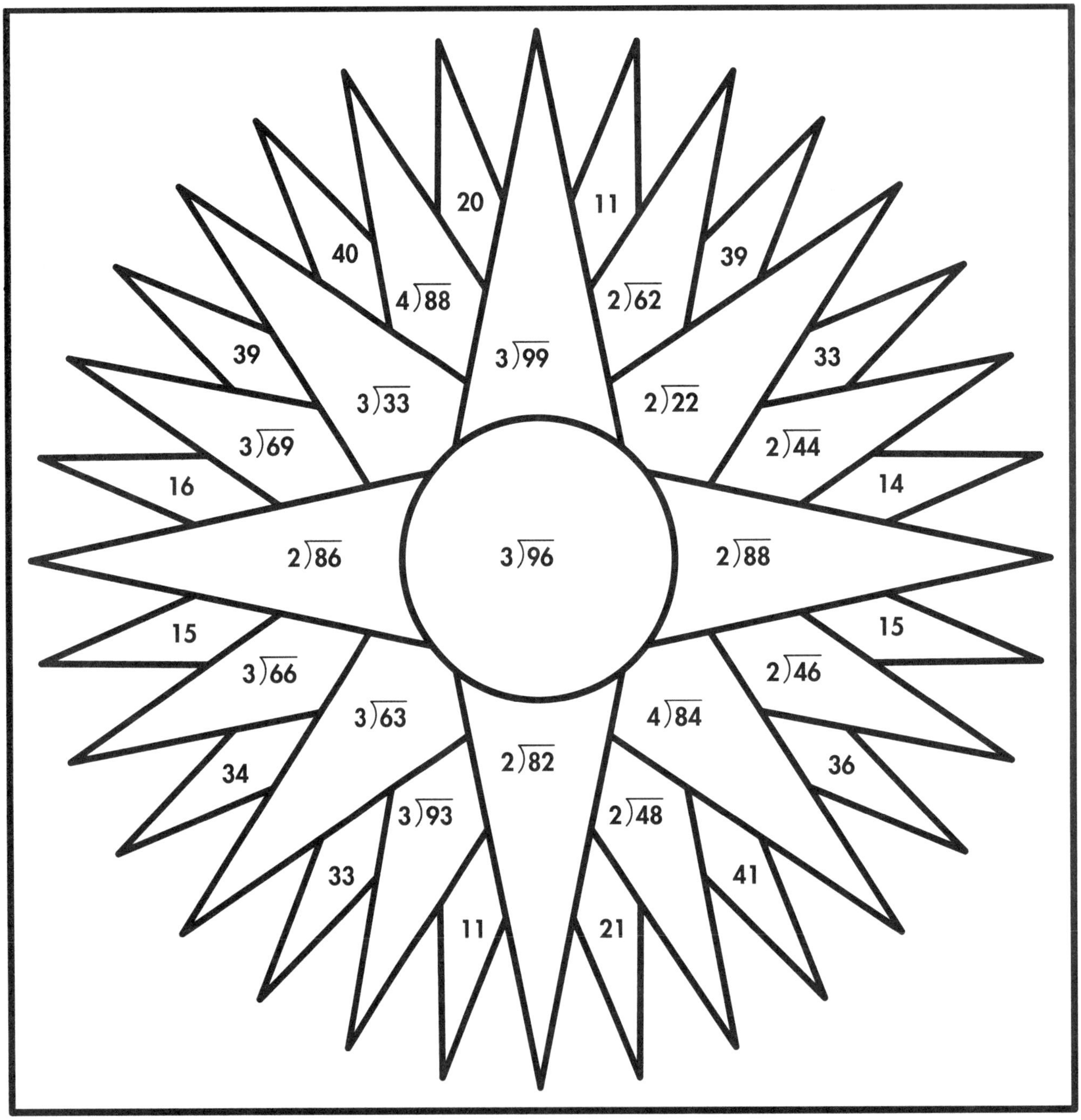

Color:

If the answer is from 11 to 21, color the space yellow.

If the answer is from 22 to 31, color the space red.

If the answer is from 32 to 44, color the space orange.

This pattern looks like the sun does on a very hot summer day.

C On the back of this sheet of paper, make two problems that can be divided evenly by a single digit. Give them to a friend to do.

Divide 2 digits by 1 digit. No remainder.

Secret Drawer

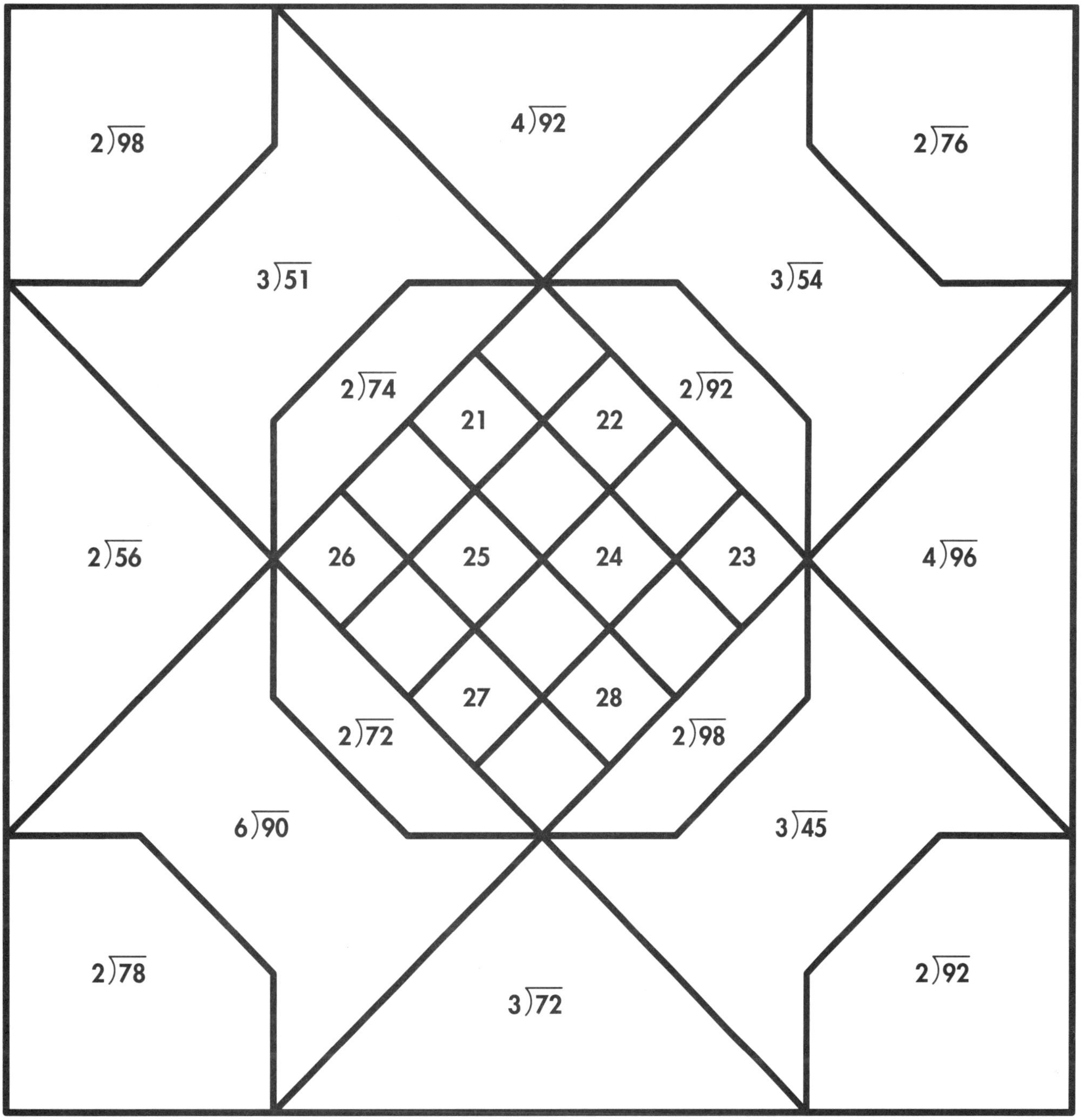

2)98	4)92	2)76
3)51		3)54
2)74	21 22	2)92
2)56	26 25 24 23	4)96
2)72	27 28	2)98
6)90		3)45
2)78	3)72	2)92

Color:

If the answer is from 11 to 20, color the space red.

If the answer is from 21 to 30, color the space orange.

If the answer is from 31 to 40, color the space green.

This pattern may have been named by a mother who kept a secret drawer filled with goodies and treasures.

C It costs $68 to rent a cabin for two days. How much does it cost each day?

Divide 2 digits by 1 digit. No remainder.

Dresden Plate

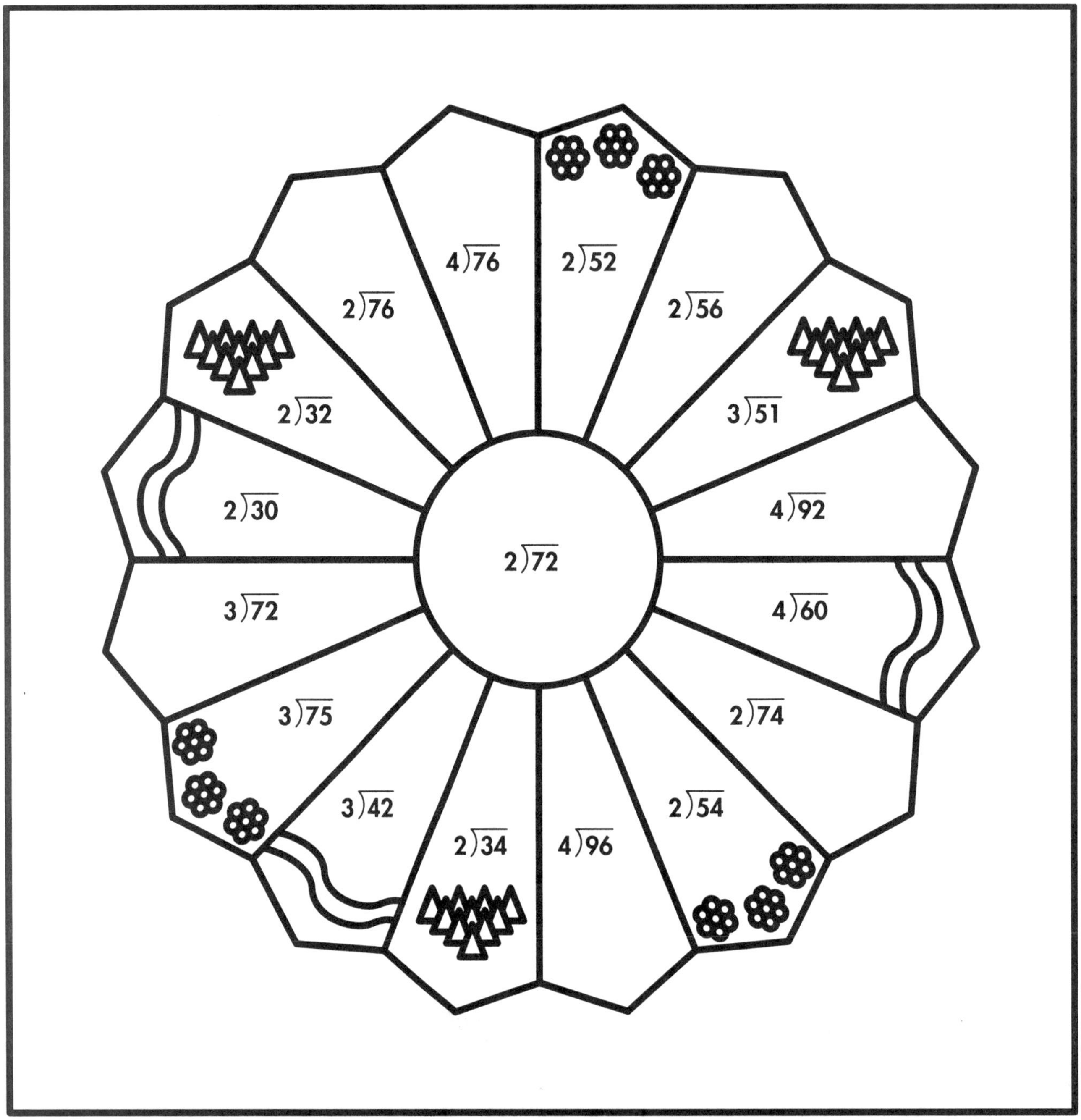

4)76 2)52

2)76 2)56

2)32 3)51

2)30 4)92

2)72

3)72 4)60

3)75 2)74

3)42 2)54

2)34 4)96

Color:

13, 14, and 15 = blue
16, 17, and 18 = red
19, 23, and 24 = yellow
25, 26, and 27 = green
28, 36, 37, and 38 = purple

This pattern was named for the design on popular dishes that came from Germany.

***C* If you want to plant thirty-six pumpkin seeds evenly in two rows, how many will you plant in each row?**

Iris

Divide 2 digits by 1 digit. Remainder.

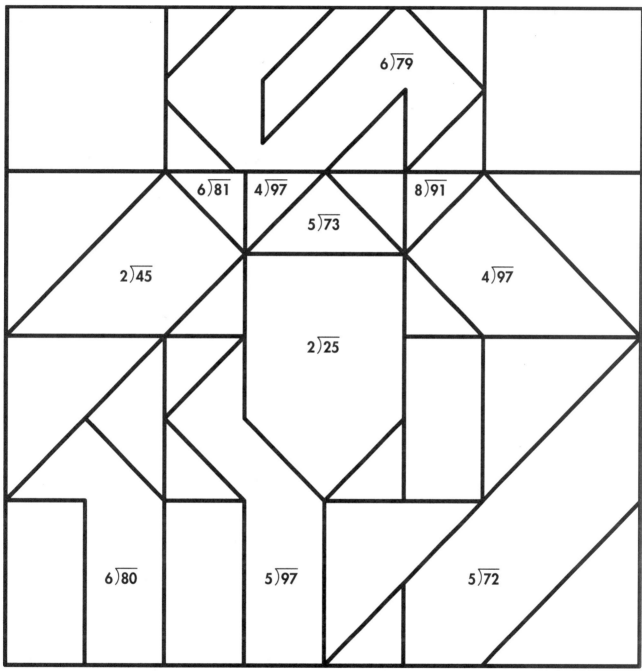

6)79

6)81 4)97 5)73 8)91

2)45 4)97

2)25

6)80 5)97 5)72

Color:

If the remainder is 1, color the space purple.
If the remainder is 2, color the space green.
If the remainder is 3, color the space pink.

Though this flower design is modern, flower patterns on quilts were very common in earlier times. Often, an engaged couple would choose their favorite flower and sew it on their marriage quilt.

***C* On the back of this sheet of paper, write the names of three flowers you like.**

Divide 2 digits by 1 digit. Remainder.

Prairie Queen

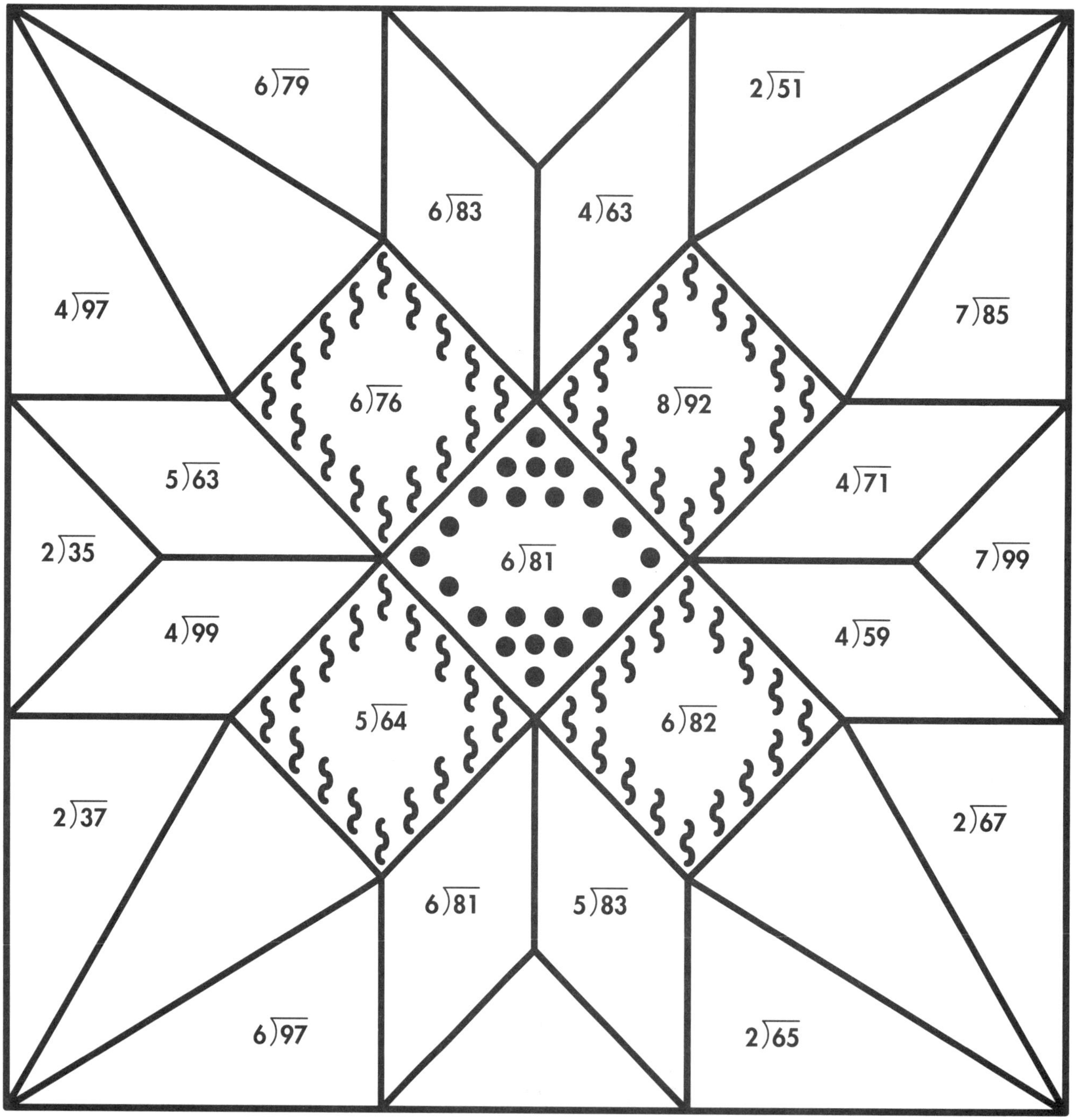

$6\overline{)79}$ $2\overline{)51}$

$6\overline{)83}$ $4\overline{)63}$

$4\overline{)97}$ $7\overline{)85}$

$6\overline{)76}$ $8\overline{)92}$

$5\overline{)63}$ $4\overline{)71}$

$2\overline{)35}$ $6\overline{)81}$ $7\overline{)99}$

$4\overline{)99}$ $4\overline{)59}$

$5\overline{)64}$ $6\overline{)82}$

$2\overline{)37}$ $2\overline{)67}$

$6\overline{)81}$ $5\overline{)83}$

$6\overline{)97}$ $2\overline{)65}$

Color:

If the remainder is 1, color the space green.

If the remainder is 4, color the space blue.

If the remainder is 3 or 5, color the space yellow.

A pioneer woman may have named this quilt pattern as she traveled across the windy prairie to her new home in the West.

***C* Divide forty-seven three times — by two, three, and four. Circle the answer with the largest remainder.**

Divide 3 digits by 1 digit. No remainder.

Crazy Ann

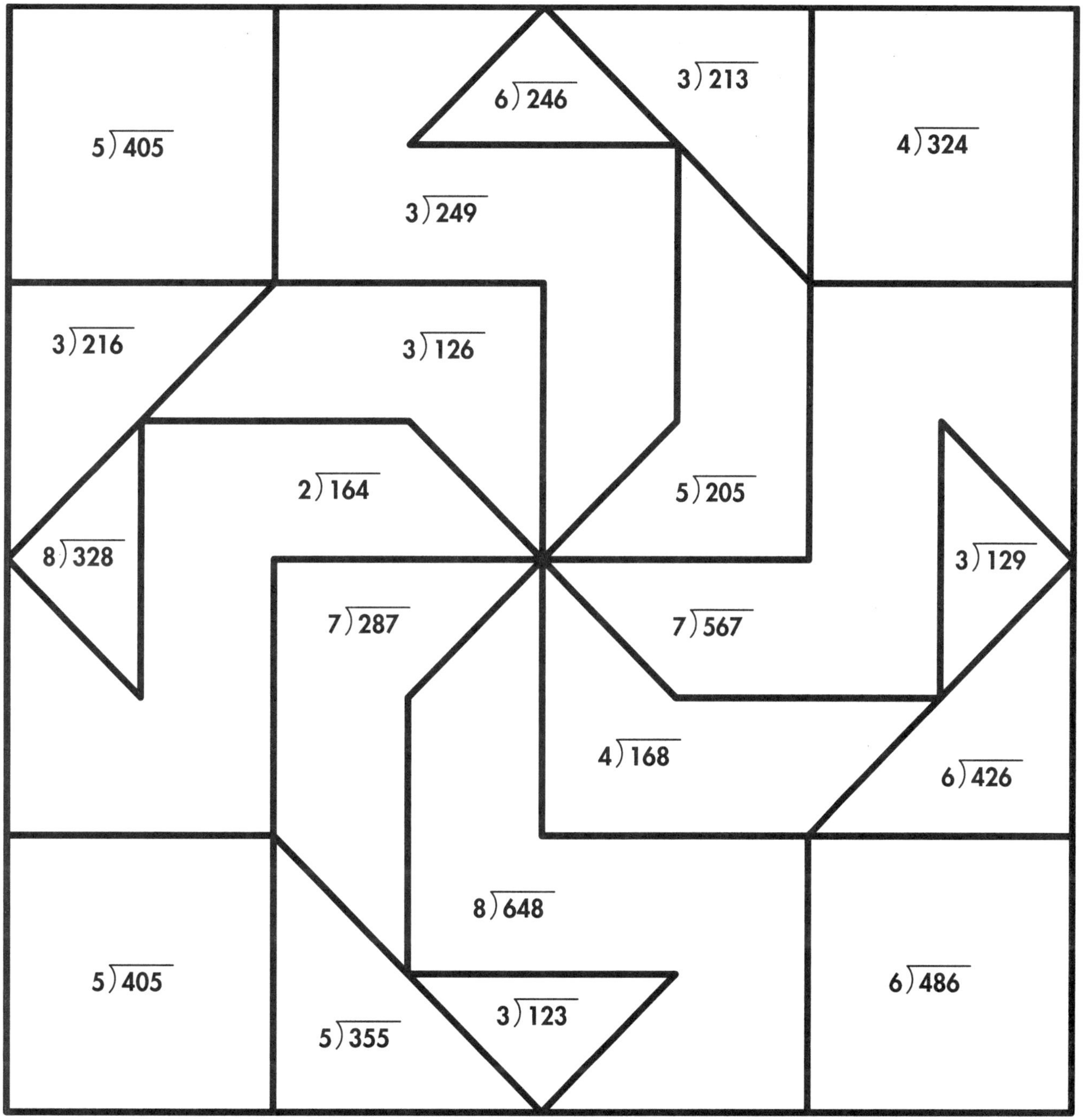

$5\overline{)405}$

$6\overline{)246}$

$3\overline{)213}$

$4\overline{)324}$

$3\overline{)249}$

$3\overline{)216}$

$3\overline{)126}$

$2\overline{)164}$

$5\overline{)205}$

$8\overline{)328}$

$3\overline{)129}$

$7\overline{)287}$

$7\overline{)567}$

$4\overline{)168}$

$6\overline{)426}$

$8\overline{)648}$

$5\overline{)405}$

$6\overline{)486}$

$3\overline{)123}$

$5\overline{)355}$

Color:

In the answer, if the tens place is 4, color the space blue.

In the answer, if the tens place is 7, color the space orange.

In the answer, if the tens place is 8, color the space brown.

Many quilts are named for family members. Ann was probably a girl who enjoyed playing jokes on her brothers and sisters.

C One hundred twenty-six fishermen need to fit into six boats. How many fishermen will be in each boat?

Divide 3 digits by 1 digit. No remainder.

Grandmother's Engagement Ring

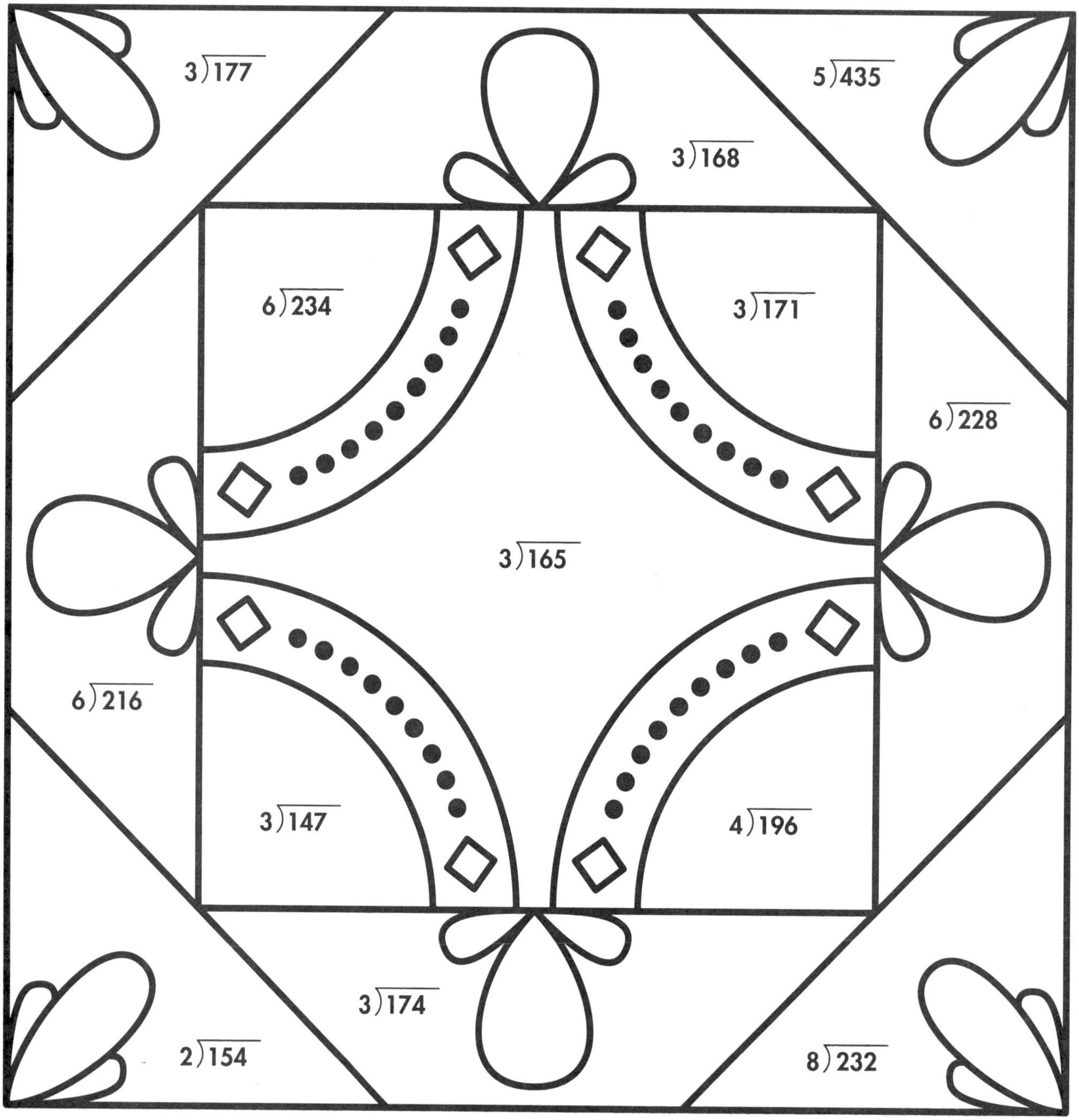

3)177

5)435

3)168

6)234

3)171

6)228

3)165

6)216

3)147

4)196

3)174

2)154

8)232

Color:

In the answer,
if the ones place is even,
color the space yellow.

In the answer,
if the ones place is odd,
color the space red.

This fancy pattern was probably designed to look like someone's favorite ring.

***C* Select one problem from this page and write it using number words instead of numerals.**

Divide 3 digits by 1 digit. Remainder.

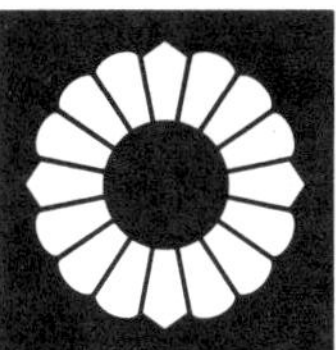

Fancy Dresden Plate

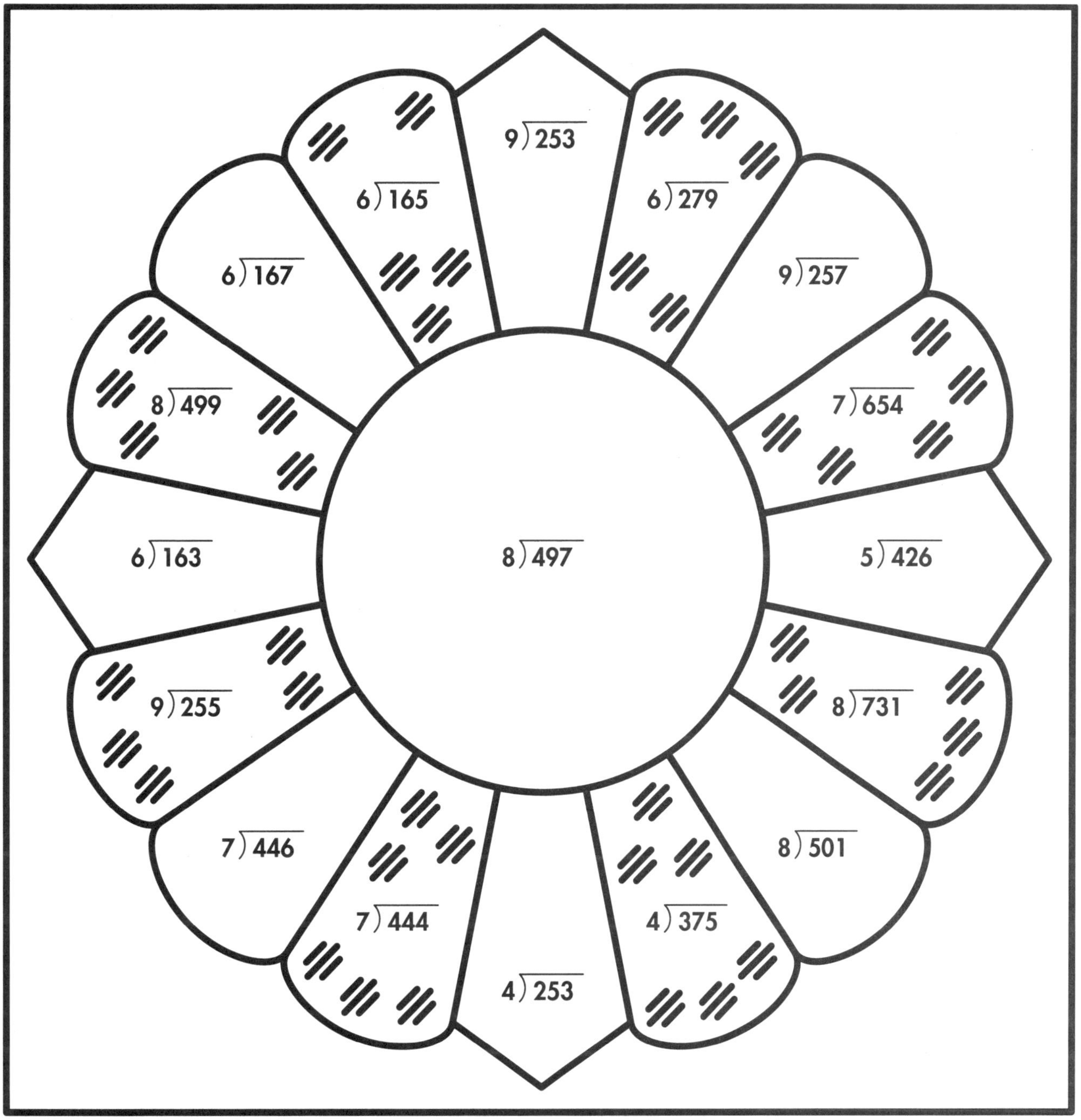

9)253

6)165

6)279

6)167

9)257

8)499

7)654

6)163

8)497

5)426

9)255

8)731

7)446

8)501

7)444

4)375

4)253

Color:

If the remainder is 1, color the space red.
If the remainder is 3, color the space blue.
If the remainder is 5, color the space yellow.

Dishes from Germany were popular in Colonial days. This pattern was special because the sides were pointed.

***C* Find your name in the phone book. Divide the page number by four. Do you have a remainder? What is it?**

Divide 3 digits by 1 digit. Remainder.

Palm Leaf

Extra Credit 5pts

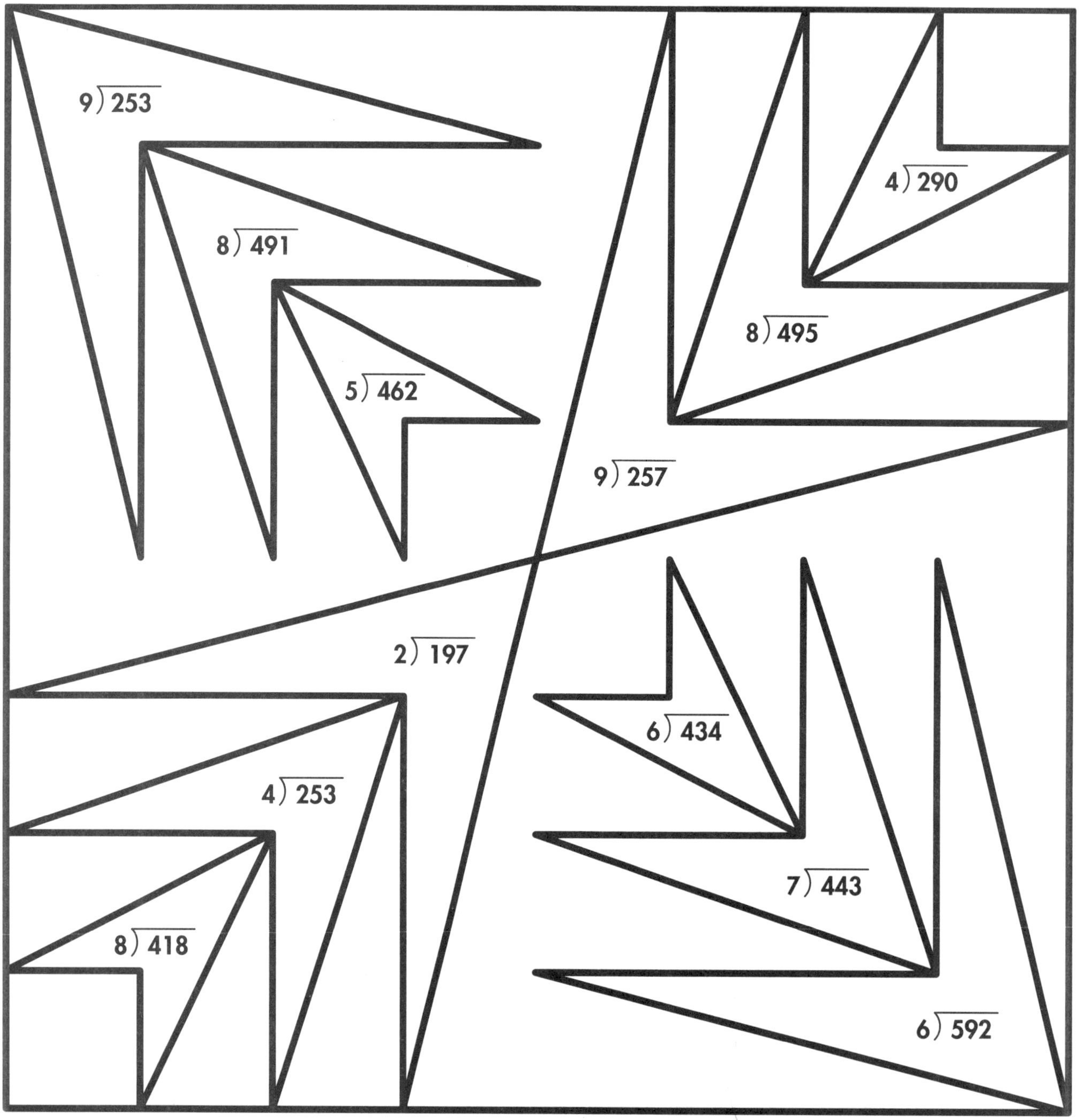

9)253

8)491

5)462

4)290

8)495

9)257

2)197

6)434

4)253

7)443

8)418

6)592

Color:

In the answer, if there is an 8 in the ones place, color the space green.

In the answer, if there is a 2 in the ones place, color the space red.

In the answer, if there is a 6 in the tens place, color the space orange.

This pattern dates back to the years before the Revolutionary War. Where might you find palm trees in this country?

____

***C* Write the dates of the Revolutionary War on the back of this sheet of paper.**

Divide 2 and 3 digits by 1 digit. Remainder.

Freedom

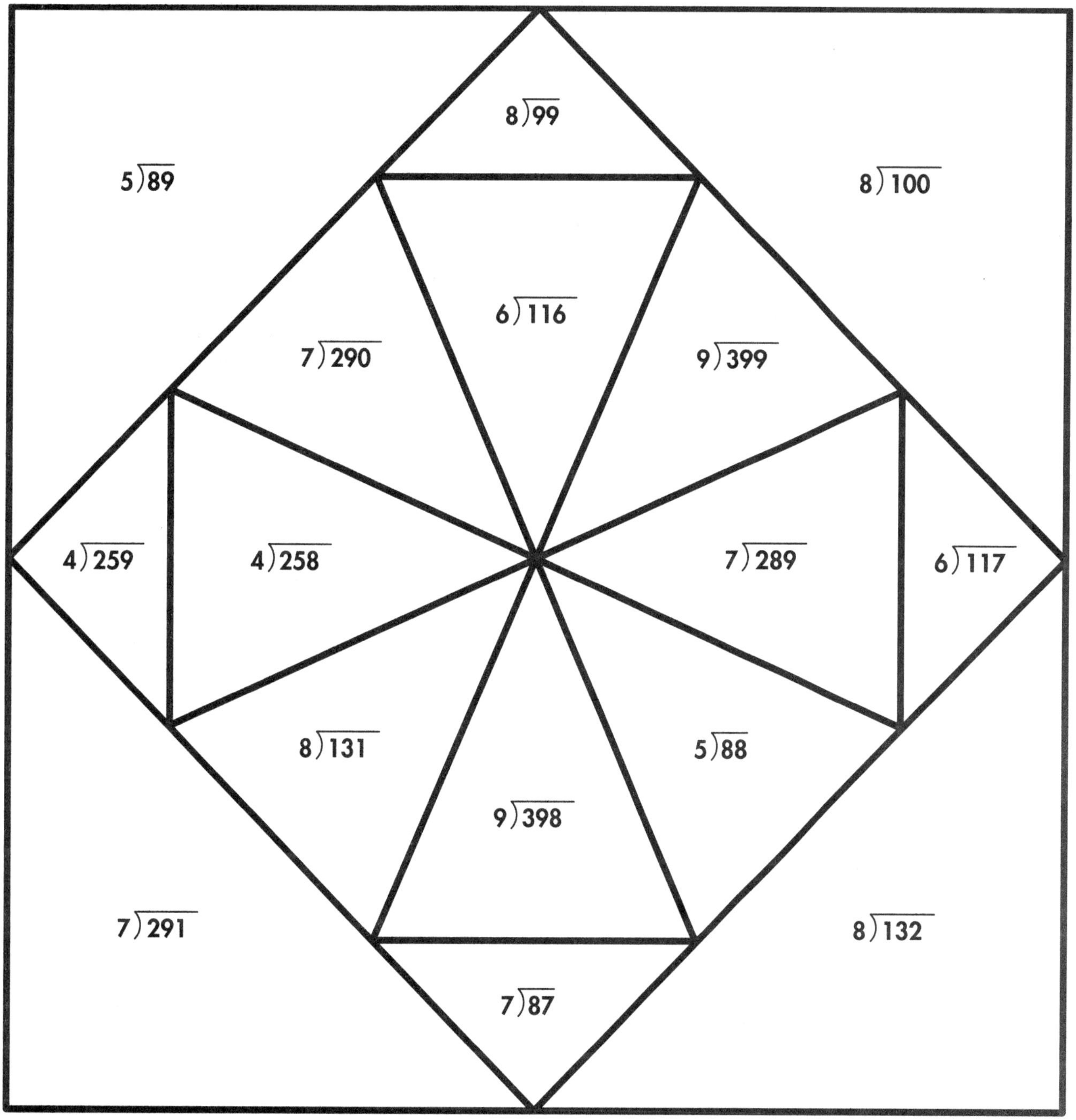

8)99

5)89

8)100

6)116

7)290

9)399

4)259

4)258

7)289

6)117

8)131

5)88

9)398

7)291

8)132

7)87

Color:

If the remainder is 2, color the space blue.
If the remainder is 3, color the space white.
If the remainder is 4, color the space red.

Quilts made of this pattern were often given to pioneer men when they turned 21.

C If each of three hundred forty-seven new houses was painted one of seven colors, how many were painted each color? Were any left over? (Each of the colors was equally represented.)

Divide 2 and 3 digits by 1 digit. Remainder.

Water Wheel

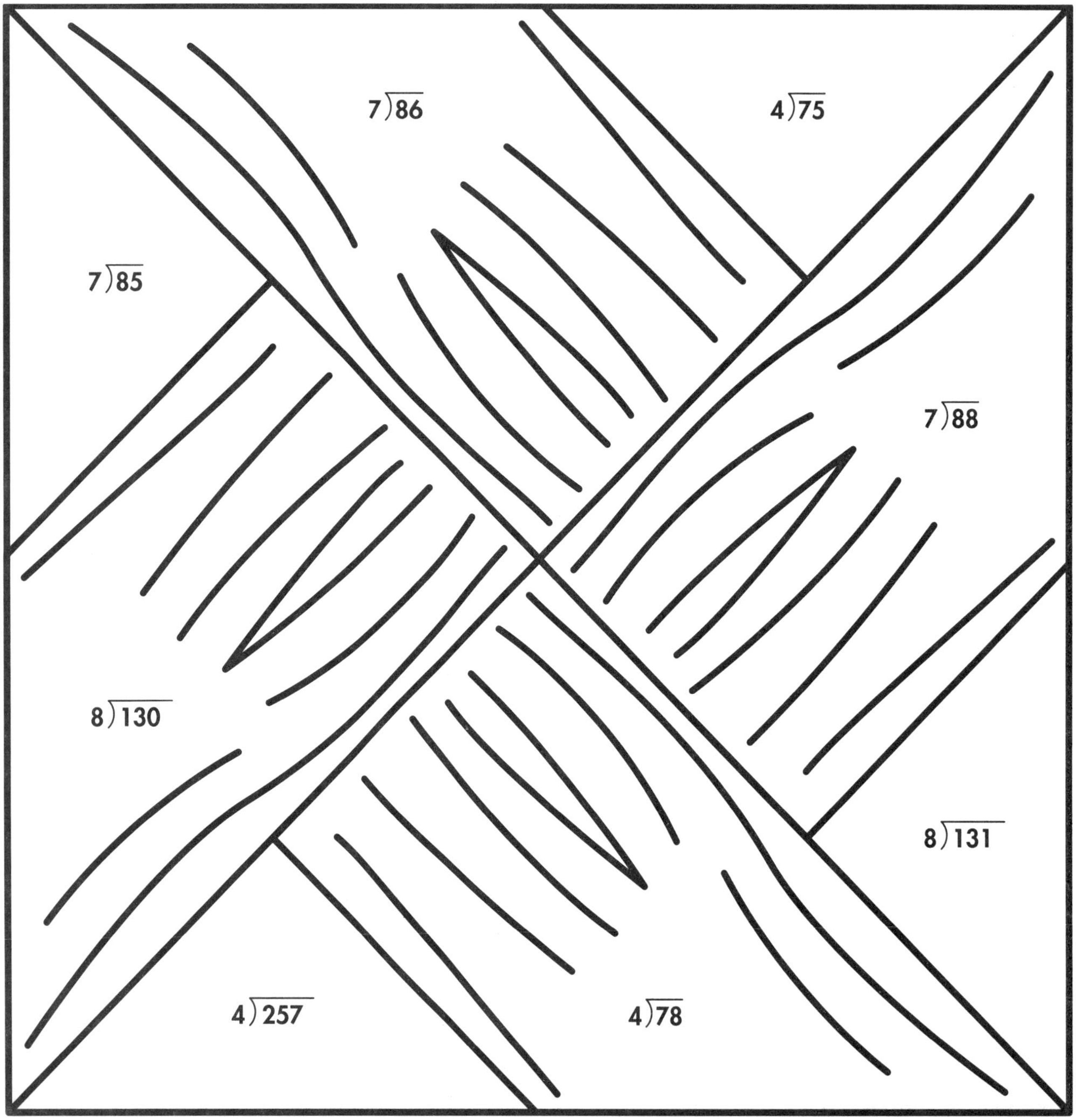

Color:

If the remainder is even, color the space brown.

If the remainder is odd, color the space white.

In this pattern you can see the four paddles of the water wheel. Water wheels were used to move boats up and down rivers.

***C* If you have seventy-nine pieces of candy and seven people to share with, how many pieces of candy will each person get? Will you have any left over?**

Divide 3 digits by 1 digit. No remainder.

Courthouse Square

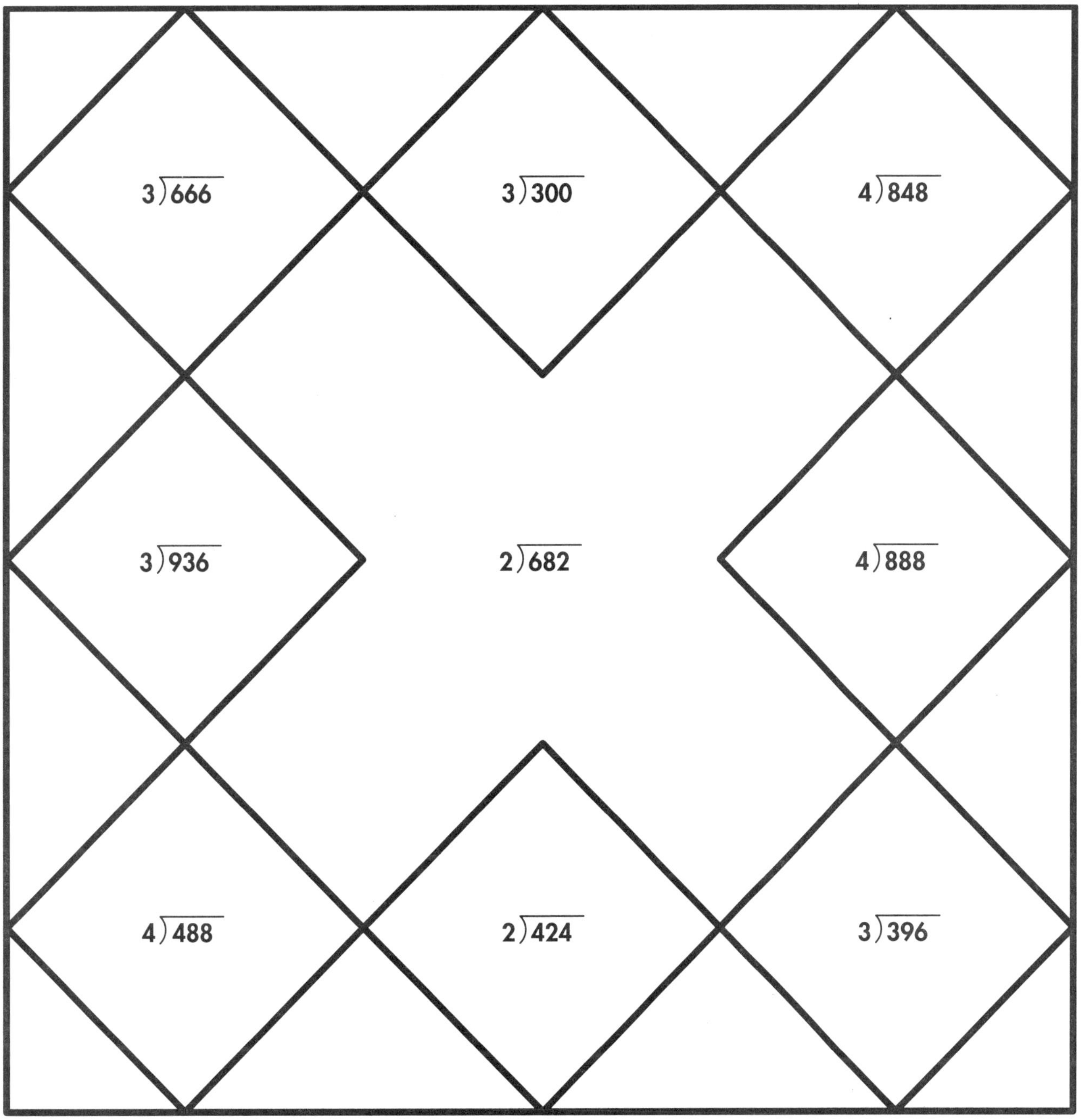

$3\overline{)666}$

$3\overline{)300}$

$4\overline{)848}$

$3\overline{)936}$

$2\overline{)682}$

$4\overline{)888}$

$4\overline{)488}$

$2\overline{)424}$

$3\overline{)396}$

Color:

If the answer is even, color the space brown.
If the answer is odd, color the space green.

This pattern looks like designs of bricks or stones you can see on some streets and in some parks.

***C* Make a division problem using three digits divided by one digit. Make sure that there is no remainder.**

Divide 3 digits by 1 digit. No remainder.

Geometric Star

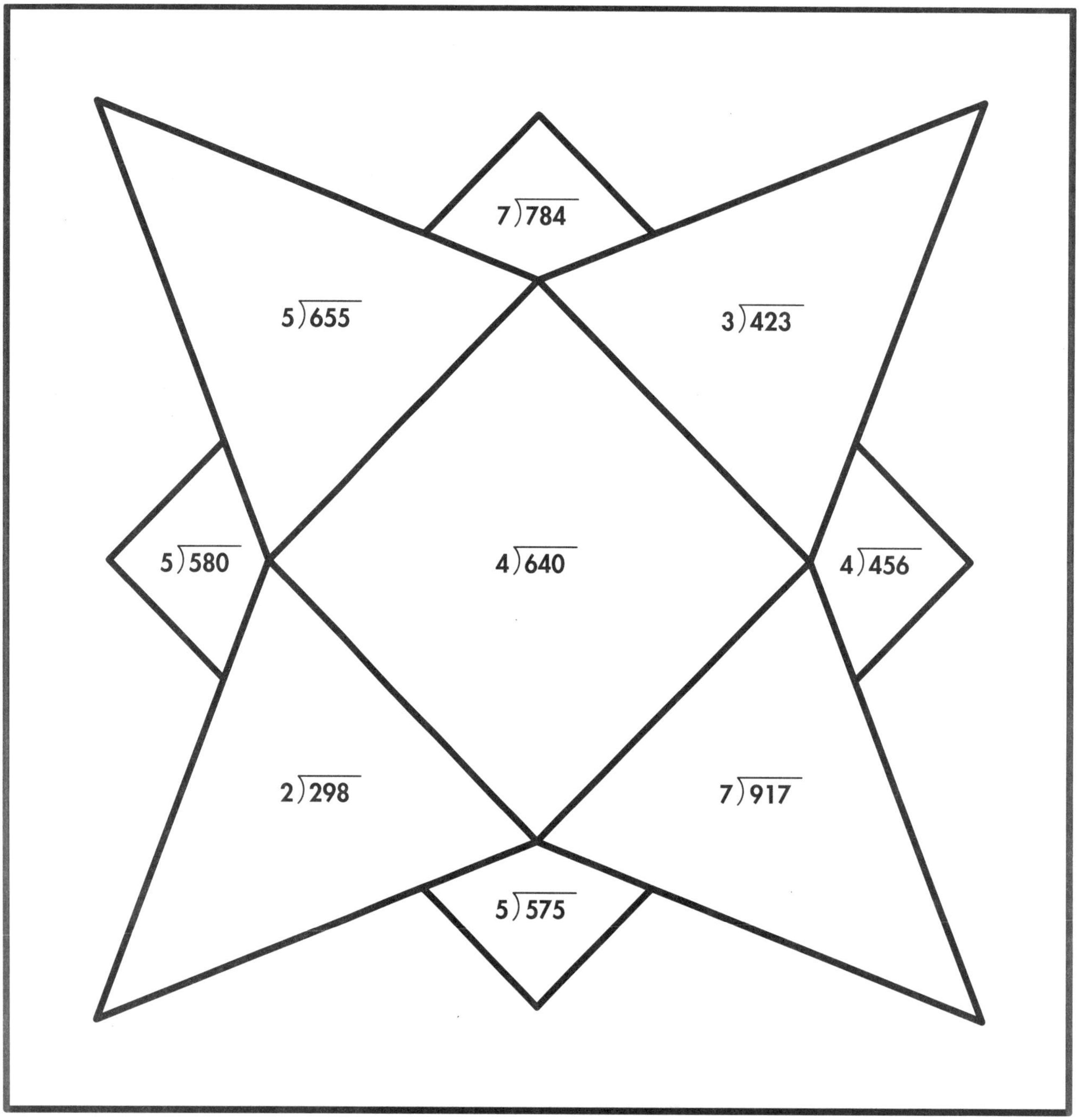

$7\overline{)784}$

$5\overline{)655}$

$3\overline{)423}$

$5\overline{)580}$

$4\overline{)640}$

$4\overline{)456}$

$2\overline{)298}$

$7\overline{)917}$

$5\overline{)575}$

Color:

If the answer is from 110 to 130, color the space blue.

If the answer is from 131 to 150, color the space yellow.

If the answer is from 151 to 160, color the space white.

Can you name the shapes that make up this star pattern?

____

C If you use two hundred sixty-four new spokes, three for each bicycle, how many bicycles can you fix?

Chips and Whetstone

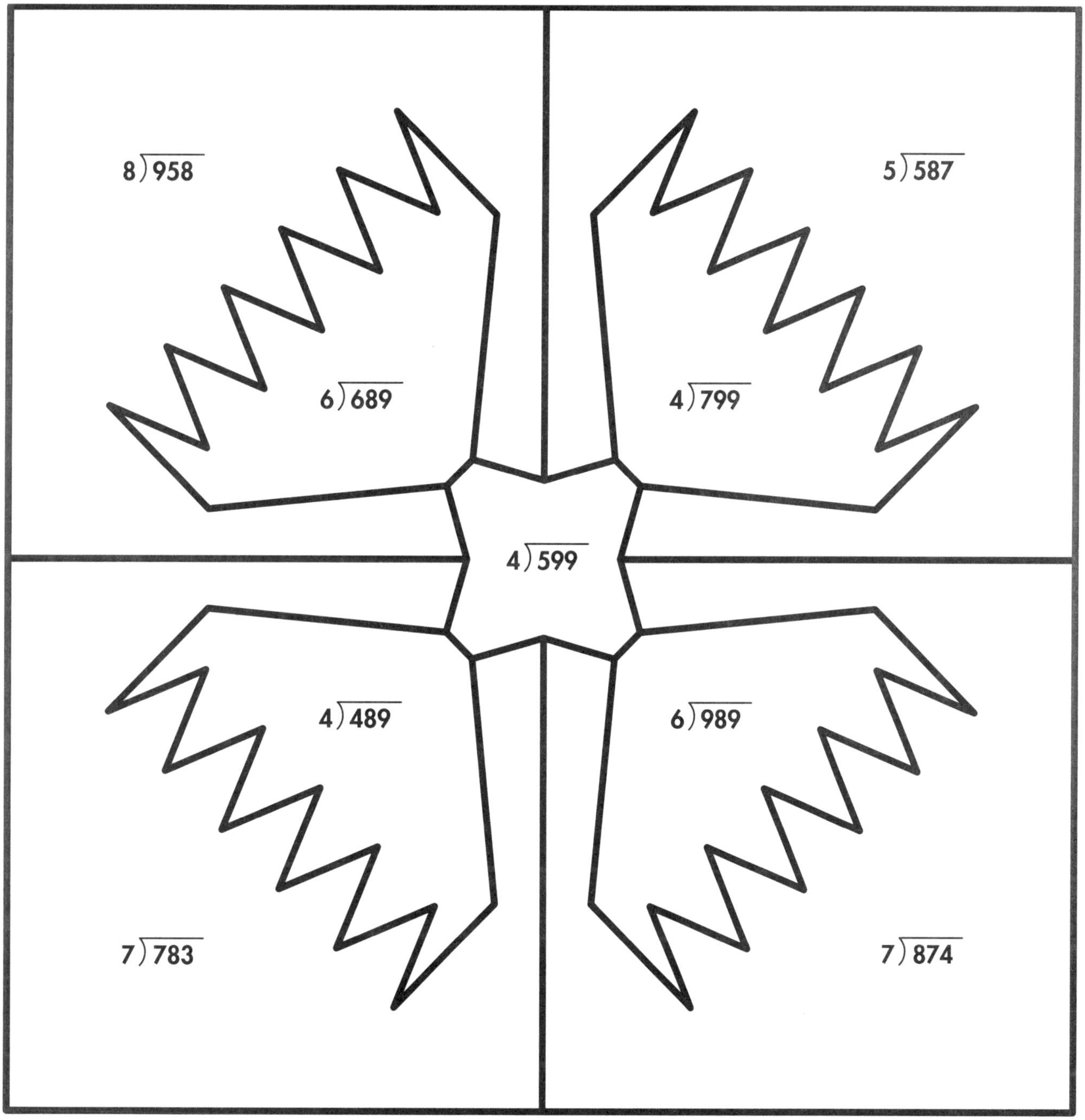

$8\overline{)958}$

$5\overline{)587}$

$6\overline{)689}$

$4\overline{)799}$

$4\overline{)599}$

$4\overline{)489}$

$6\overline{)989}$

$7\overline{)783}$

$7\overline{)874}$

Color:

If the remainder is odd, color the space brown.

If the remainder is even, color the space yellow.

People sharpen knives and blades on special pieces of stone, called whetstones. Sometimes the stones were shaped like this.

***C* If you set up four hundred thirty-five chairs in rows of eight, will there be any extra chairs?**

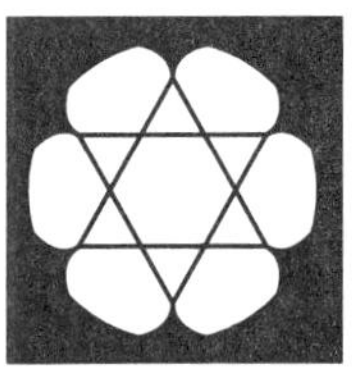

Divide 3 digits by 1 digit. Zero in quotient.

Star and Planets

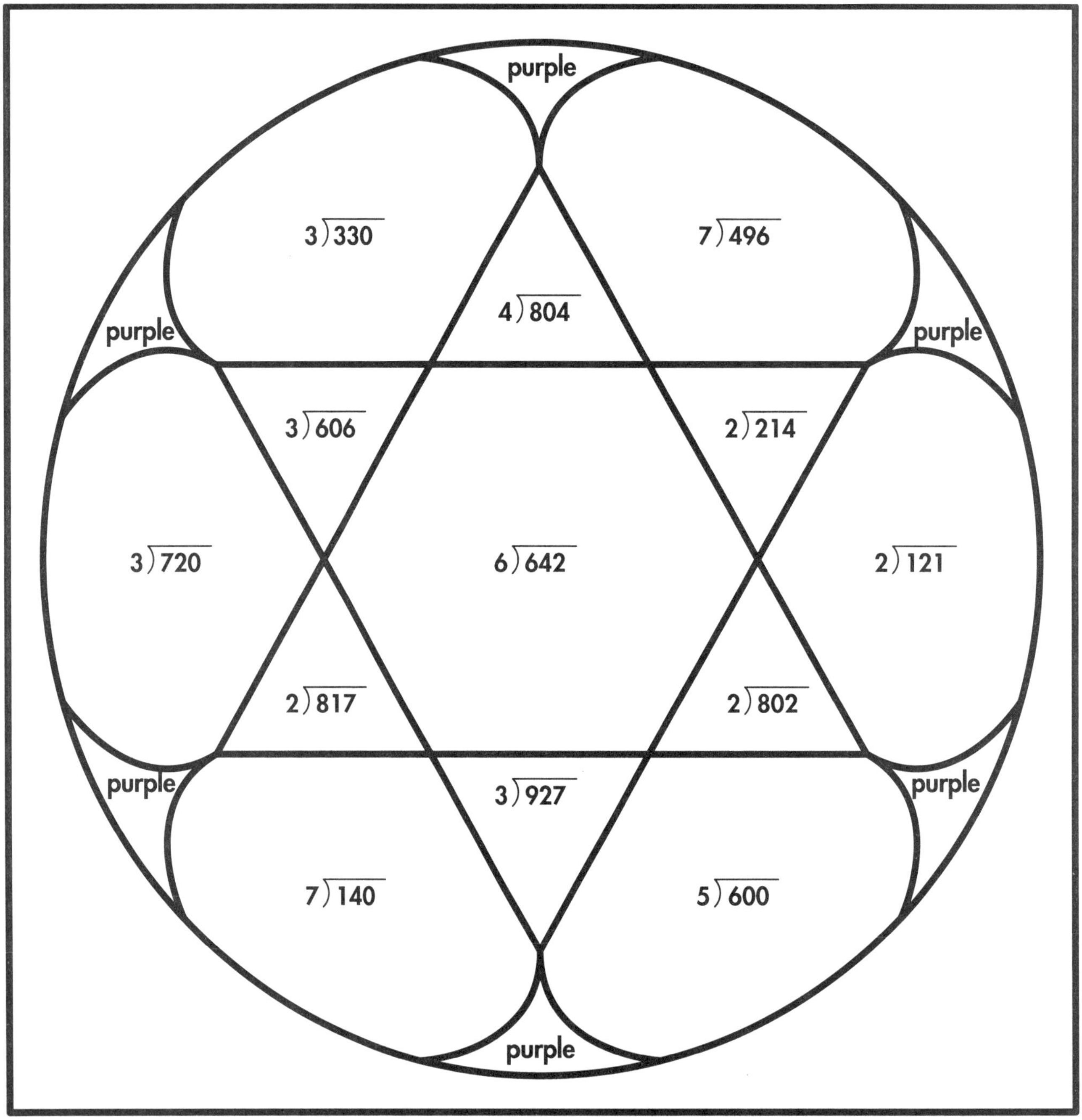

Color:

In the answer, if there is a 0 in the tens place, color the space yellow.

In the answer, if there is a 0 in the ones place, color the space green.

Look closely. Can you see six planets clustered around the star?

***C* Write the names of four planets on the back of this sheet of paper.**

Divide 3 digits by 2 digits. Remainder.

Five-Pointed Star

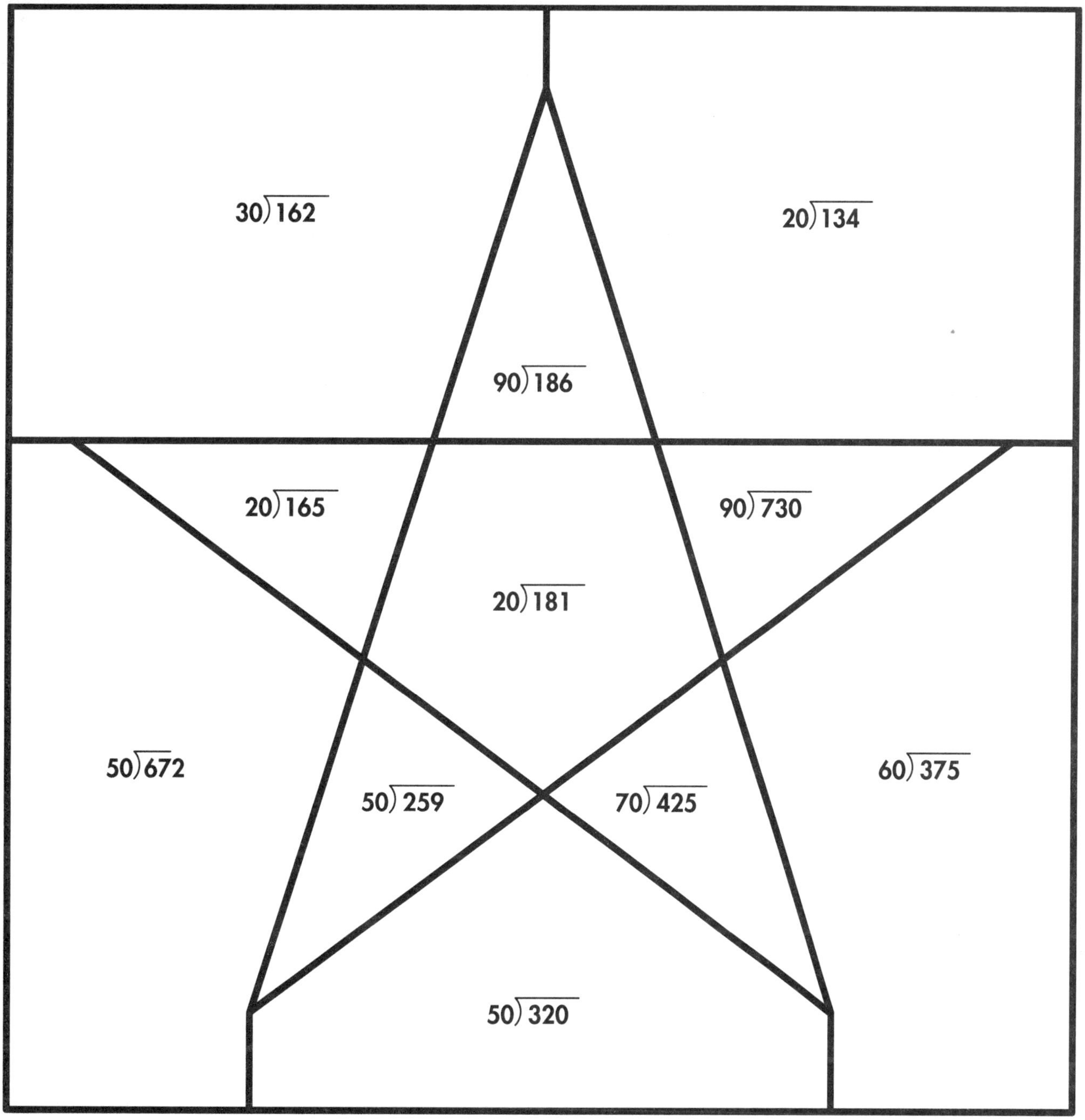

30)162

20)134

90)186

20)165

90)730

20)181

50)672

50)259

70)425

60)375

50)320

Color:

If the remainder is from 1 to 10, color the space red.

If the remainder is from 11 to 20, color the space black.

Star pictures are popular for quilt patterns.

C On the back of this sheet of paper, write the names of three things that have stars in their designs.

Divide 2 and 3 digits by 2 digits. Remainder.

Ribbon Block

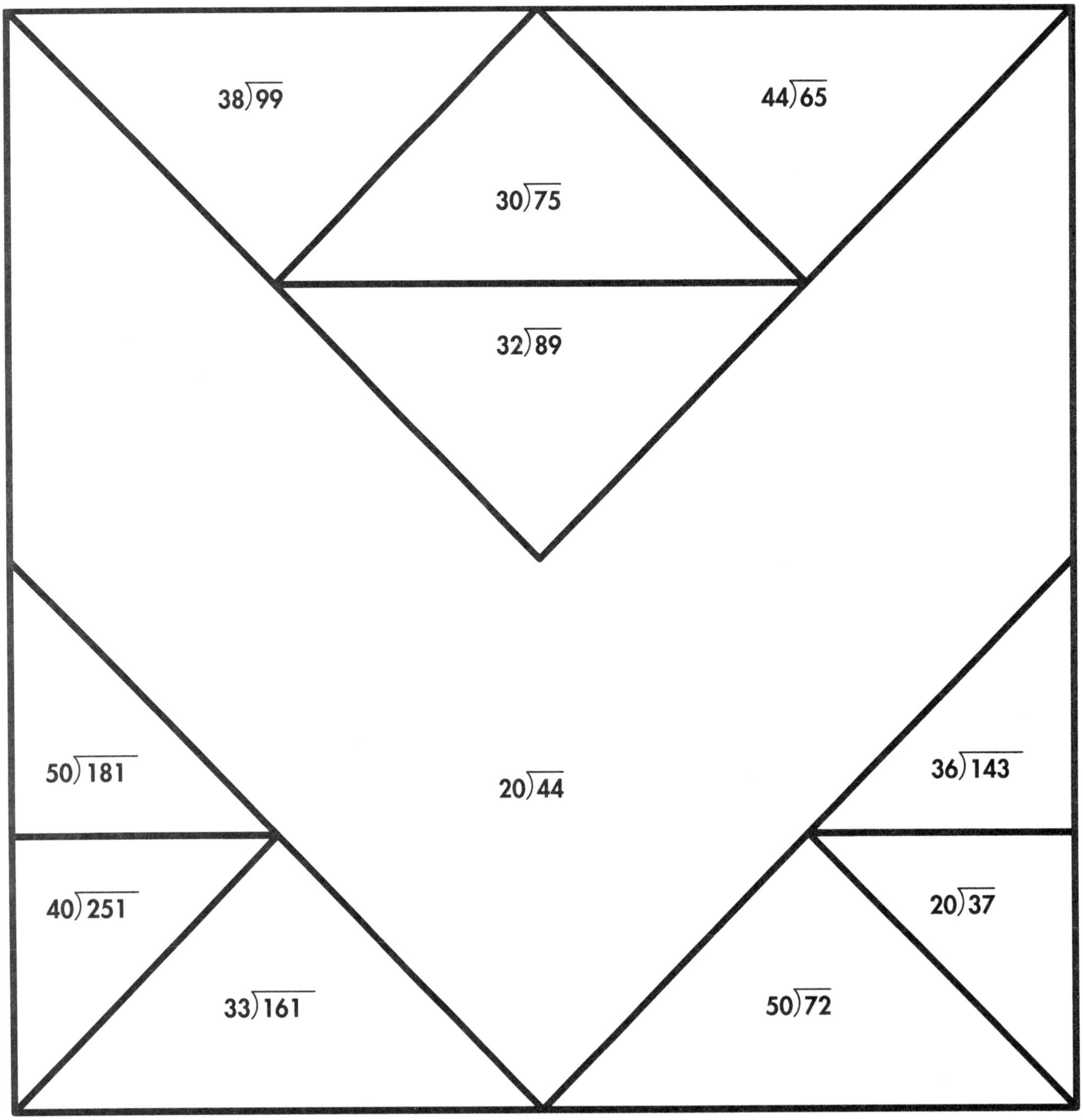

$38\overline{)99}$

$44\overline{)65}$

$30\overline{)75}$

$32\overline{)89}$

$50\overline{)181}$

$20\overline{)44}$

$36\overline{)143}$

$40\overline{)251}$

$20\overline{)37}$

$33\overline{)161}$

$50\overline{)72}$

Color:

If the remainder is from 1 to 10, color the space red.

If the remainder is from 11 to 20, color the space blue.

If the remainder is from 21 to 35, color the space yellow.

Sometimes quilt squares were sewn with pieces of ribbon instead of pieces of cloth. This was a favorite ribbon pattern.

***C* Name a material in your home that could be used to make into a quilt square.**

Divide 3 digits by 2 digits. Remainder.

String Block

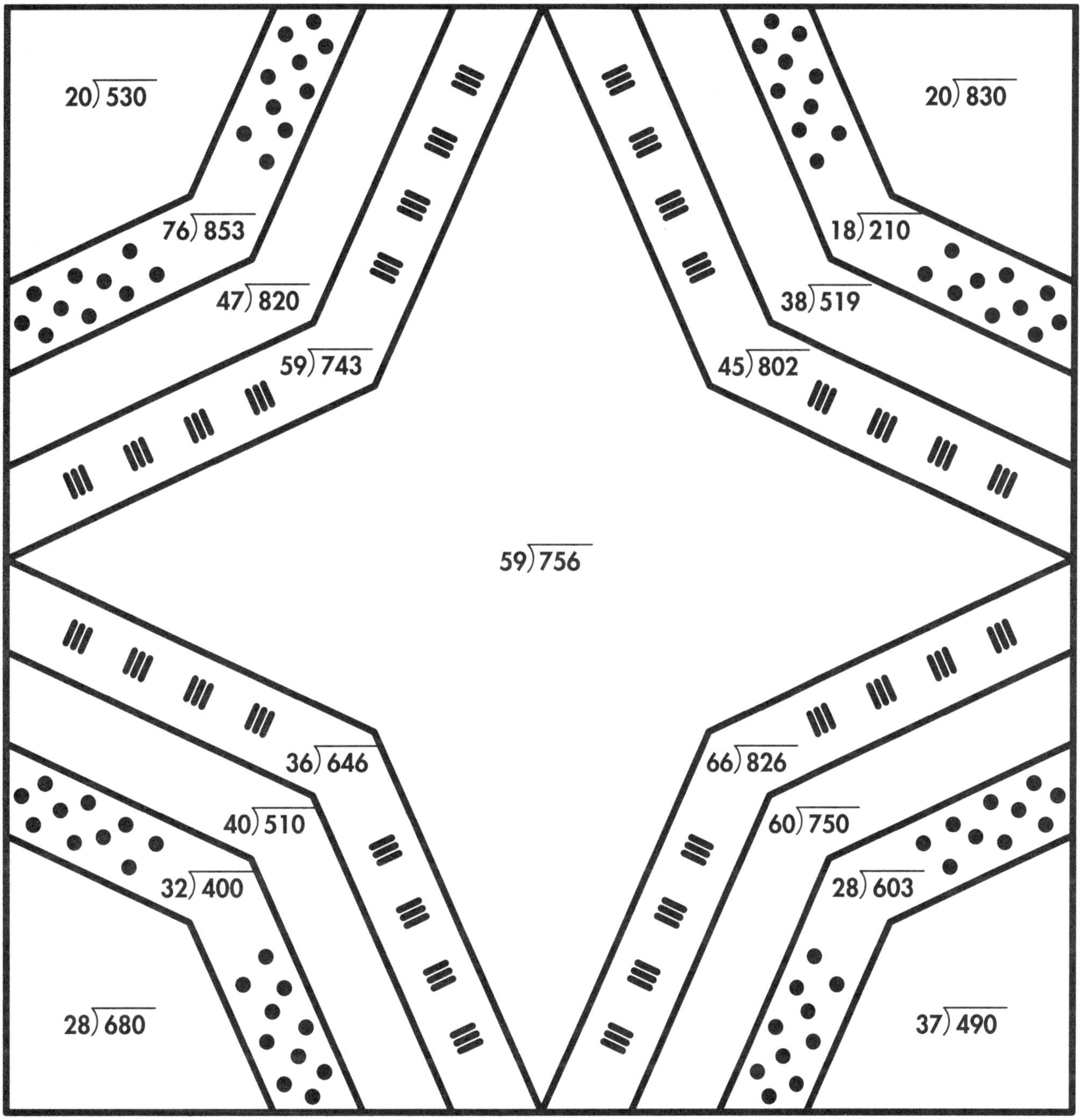

Color:

If the remainder is from:

1 to 10 – red
11 to 20 – orange
21 to 30 – yellow
31 to 40 – green
41 to 50 – blue

Long and skinny silk neckties were used to make this design.

C If eight hundred sixty-seven tourists are going to the Grand Canyon and they have to divide into groups of nineteen, how many groups will there be?

Baby's Blocks

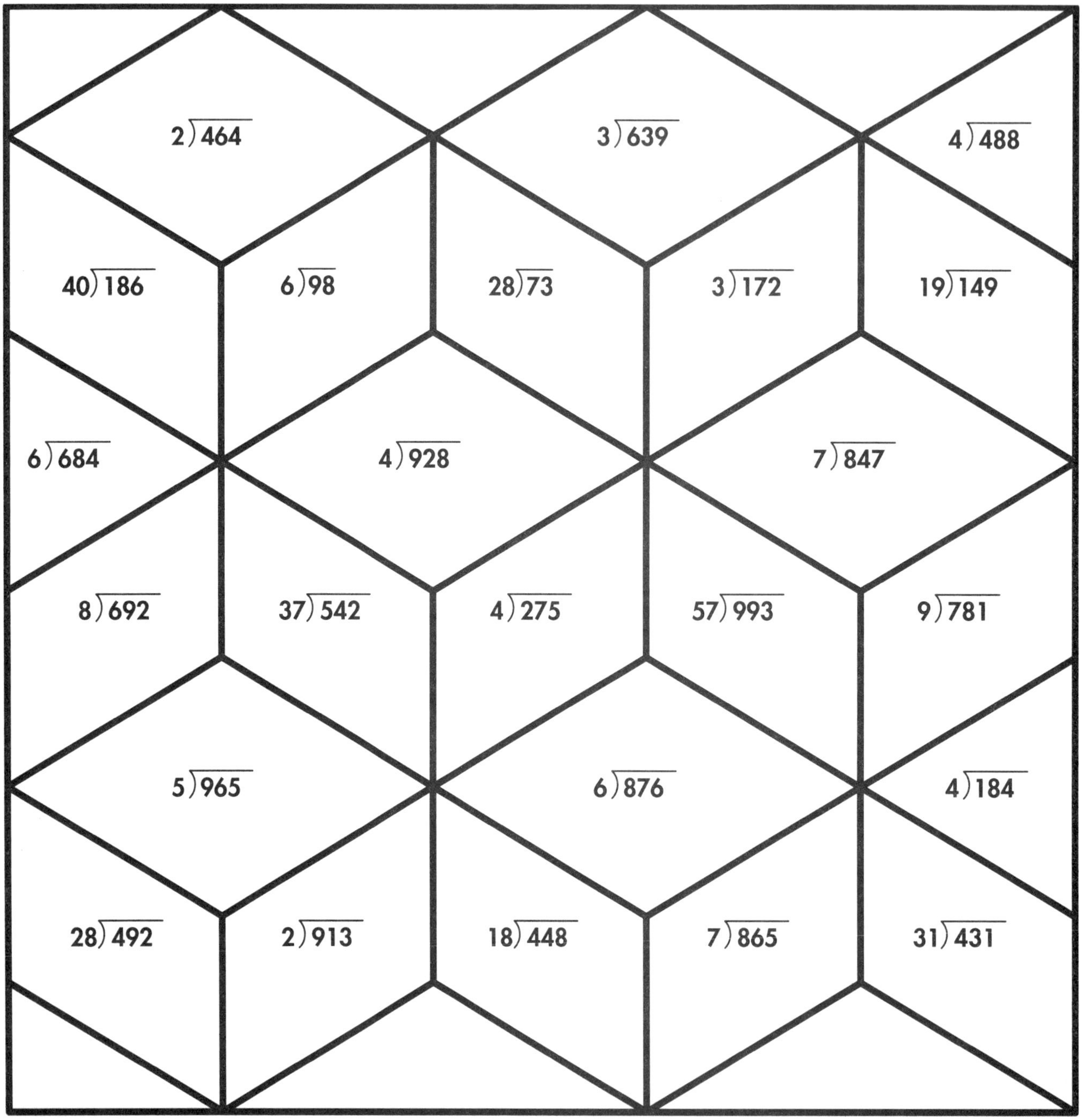

Mixed division.

2)464

3)639

4)488

40)186

6)98

28)73

3)172

19)149

6)684

4)928

7)847

8)692

37)542

4)275

57)993

9)781

5)965

6)876

4)184

28)492

2)913

18)448

7)865

31)431

Color:

If there is no remainder, color the space yellow.

If the remainder is from 1 to 15, color the space blue.

If the remainder is from 16 to 30, color the space green.

This picture resembles building blocks that children play with.

C An airplane has a crew of nine and two hundred fifty-five passengers. One-fourth of the people will deplane in Florida. How many people will get off the plane?

Creative activity

Goose in the Pond

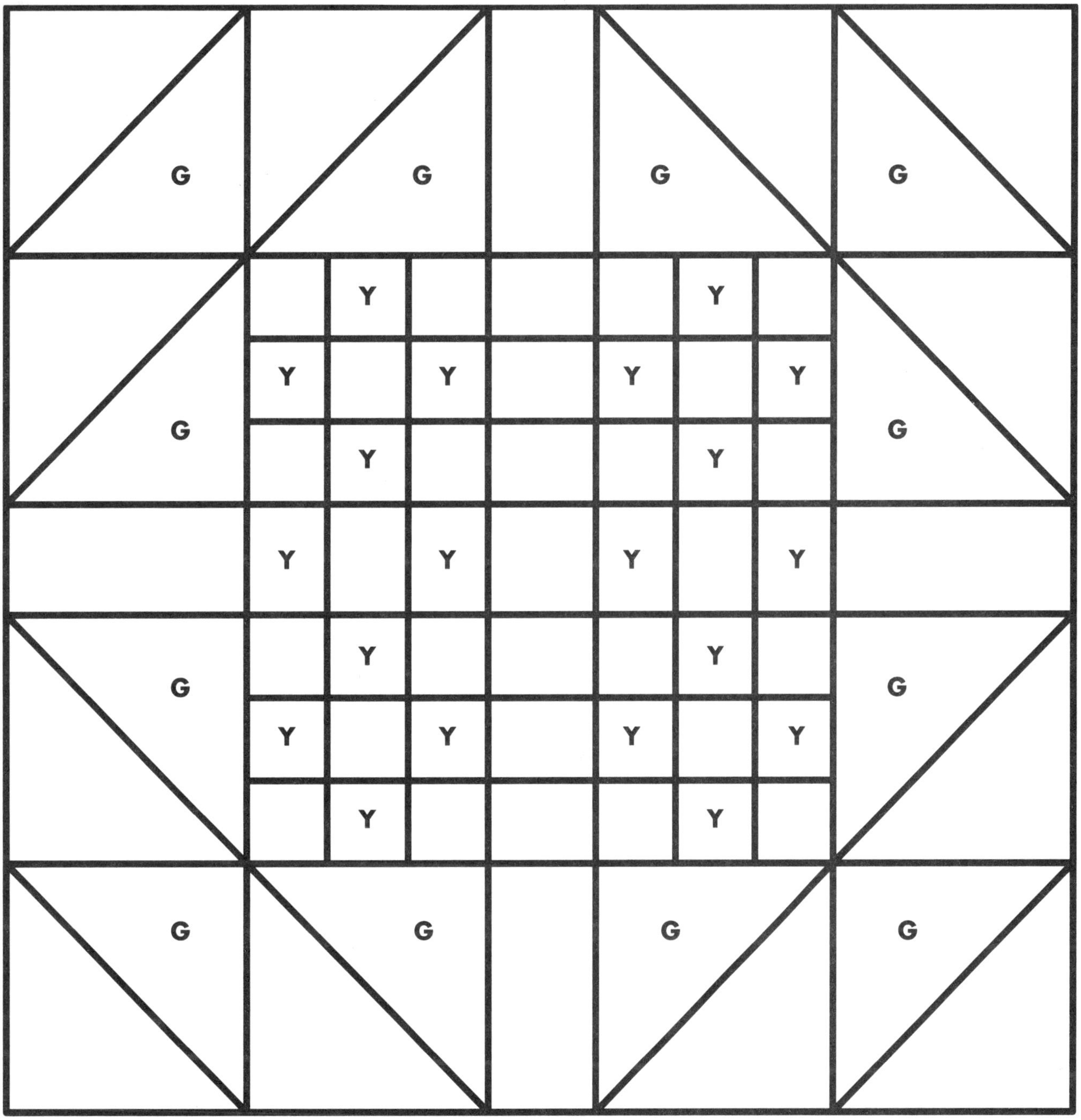

Create a color code using facts selected by your teacher.
Use the colors green (G) and yellow (Y).

Symbol

Quilt
Name: ______________________________

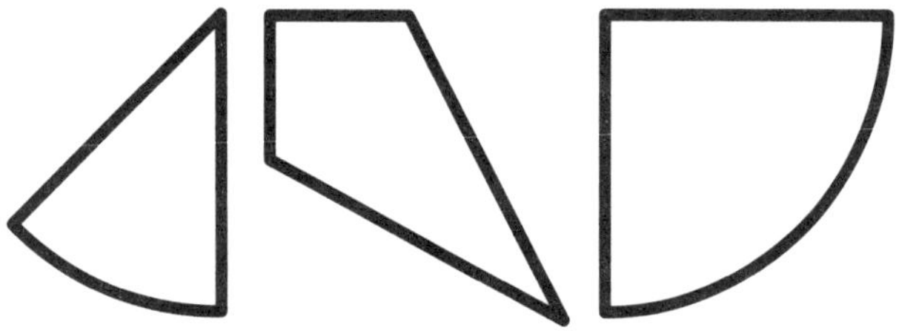

Use these shapes to draw a pattern with a flower design. Name the pattern and give a meaning for the name you have chosen.

Resources

Lenice Ingram Bacon: *Quilting*

Dolores A. Hinson: *A Quilter's Companion*

Dolores A. Hinson: *Quilting Manual*

Marguerite Ickis: *The Standard Book of Quilt-Making and Collecting*

Bonnie Leman: *Quick and Easy Quilting*

Maggie Malone: *One Hundred Fifteen Classic American Patchwork Quilt Patterns*

Ruby Mckim: *One Hundred and One Patchwork Patterns*

About the Author

Graule Studio

Debra Baycura has been an elementary school teacher for 15 years. She studied at Indiana University of Pennsylvania and Slippery Rock University, and is currently working on an Elementary Principal Certificate at Westminster College.

Debra lives with her husband and three children in New Brighton, Pennsylvania. She says, "Although I have never made a quilt, the designs and history of American quilts fascinate me."